1

Stand Out

Standards-Based English

Rob Jenkins

Staci Lyn Sabbagh

Australia • Canada • Mexico • Singapore • Spain • United Kingdom • United States

Stand Out 1

Standards-Based English

by Rob Jenkins and Staci Lyn Sabbagh

Acquisitions Editor
Sherrise Roehr

Managing Editor
James W. Brown

Developmental Editor
Ingrid Wisniewska

Associate Developmental Editor
Sarah Barnicle

Editorial Assistant
Elizabeth Allen

Marketing Manager
Eric Bredenberg

Director, Global ESL Training & Development
Evelyn Nelson

Production Editor
Jeff Freeland

Senior Manufacturing Coordinator
Mary Beth Hennebury

Project Manager
Maryellen Killeen

Compositor
TSI Graphics

Text Printer/Binder
Banta

Cover Printer
Phoenix Color Corporation

Designers
Elise Kaiser
Julia Gecha

Cover Designer
Gina Petti

Illustrators
James Edwards represented by Sheryl Beranbaum
Vilma Ortiz-Dillon
Scott MacNeill

Cover Art
Diana Ong/SuperStock

Printed in the U. S. A.
3 4 5 6 7 8 9 06 05 04 03 02

For more information, contact Heinle Publishers, 25 Thomson Place, Boston, MA 02210; or find us on the World Wide Web at: www.heinle.com

Library of Congress Catalog-in-Publication Data

Jenkins, Rob.
Stand out 1 : standards-based English / by Rob Jenkins and Staci Lyn Sabbagh.
p. cm.
Includes index.
ISBN 0-8384-2214-4
1. English language—Textbooks for foreign speakers. I. Title: Stand out one. II. Sabbagh, Staci Lyn. III. Title.

PE1128 .J434 2002
428.2'4—dc21

2001051991

PHOTO CREDITS

Front Matter:
Page v: Courtney Sabbagh

Pre-Unit:
Page P2: Top: Gary Connor/PhotoEdit; Michael Newman/PhotoEdit; Bottom: Mark Richards/PhotoEdit; Jonathan Nourok/PhotoEdit
Page P3: Mark Richards/PhotoEdit; Johnathan Nourok/PhotoEdit
Page P5: Top:©Steve Cole/PhotoDisk/PictureQuest; ©Corbis Images/PictureQuest Bottom: Bonnie Kamin/PhotoEdit/PictureQuest; Bob Daemmrich/The Image Works

Unit 1:
Page 2: Top: Michael Newman/PhotoEdit; Jonathan Nourok/PhotoEdit Bottom: Michael Newman/PhotoEdit; Mark Richards/PhotoEdit
Page 5: Top: Michael Newman/PhotoEdit; Jonathan Nourok/PhotoEdit; Michael Newman/PhotoEdit Bottom: Gary Connor/PhotoEdit; Digital Vision/PictureQuest; Michael Freeman/PhotoEdit
Page 6: Gary Connor/PhotoEdit; Jonathan Nourok/PhotoEdit; Michael Newman/PhotoEdit
Page 13: Top: Bettman/CORBIS; Right: Jean Coughlin; Middle: Jean Coughlin; Bottom: Corbis Images/PictureQuest; Jose Carrillo/PhotoEdit; Corbis Images/PictureQuest
Page 15: Jean Coughlin all except Center: Spencer Grant/PhotoEdit
Page 18: Jean Coughlin

Unit 2:
Page 23: Jean Coughlin
Page 24: Top: Heinle & Heinle; Middle: Heinle & Heinle and Jean Coughlin; Bottom: Jean Coughlin
Page 30: Top: Jean Coughlin; Far Right: Erv Schowengerdt; Middle and Bottom: Jean Coughlin

Unit 3:
Page 42: Jean Coughlin
Page 49: Top: Jean Coughlin; Bottom Jean Coughlin; Right: Erv Schowengerdt
Page 54: Left Jean Coughlin; Center and Right: Erv Schowengerdt

Unit 4:
Page 64: Jean Coughlin
Page 68: Michael Newman/PhotoEdit; Billl Aron/PhotoEdit; Michael Newman/PhotoEdit; Erv Schowengerdt

Unit 6:
Page 108: Top: Dennis Brack/Black Star Publishing/PictureQuest; David Young-Wolff/PhotoEdit Bottom: Donna Day/Stone/Getty Images; Felicia Martinez/PhotoEdit
Page 110: Julian Calder/Stone Images; Tom Carter/PhotoEdit; Dana White/PhotoEdit
Page 115: Michael Freeman/PhotoEdit; Mark Richards/PhotoEdit; Rhoda Sidney/PhotoEdit; David Young-Wolf/PhotoEdit

Unit 7:
Page 121: Richard Hutchins/PhotoEdit; Michael Newman/PhotoEdit; Stephen Frisch/Stock, Boston/PictureQuest; Bill Aron/PhotoEdit; Michael Newman/PhotoEdit
Page 125: David Young-Wolff/PhotoEdit/PictureQuest
Page 128: Top: Jean Coughlin; Jean Coughlin; David Young-Wolff/PhotoEdit; Jean Coughlin; Heinle & Heinle
Page 130: Jean Coughlin
Page 137: Michael Newman/PhotoEdit; Michael Newman/PhotoEdit; Stephen Frisch/Stock, Boston/PictureQuest

Unit 8:
Page 143: Corbis Images/PictureQuest; Bob Daemmrich/The Image Works; Jean Coughlin; Bonnie Kamin/PhotoEdit/PictureQuest; Anton Vengo/SuperStock; Frank Siteman/Stock, Boston, Inc./PictureQuest
Page 151: Pictor International/Pictor International Ltd./PictureQuest; Walter Hodges/CORBIS; Michael Newman/PhotoEdit/PictureQuest; David Young-Wolf/PhotoEdit; Jonathan Nourok/PhotoEdit; Michael Newman/PhotoEdit
Page 152: David Kelly Crow/PhotoEdit; David Young-Wolff/PhotoEdit; Rachel Epstein/The Image Works

ACKNOWLEDGMENTS

The authors and publisher would like to thank the following reviewers, consultants, and participants in focus groups:

Elizabeth Aderman
(New York City Board of Education, New York, NY)

Shannon Bailey
(Austin Community College, Austin, TX)

Sharon Baker
(Roseville Adult School, Roseville, CA)

Lillian Barredo
(Stockton School for Adults, Stockton, CA)

Linda Boice
(Elk Grove Adult Education, Elk Grove, CA)

Chan Bostwick
(Los Angeles Unified School District, Los Angeles, CA)

Rose Cantu
(John Jay High School, San Antonio, TX)

Toni Chapralis
(Fremont School for Adults, Sacramento, CA)

Melanie Chitwood
(Miami-Dade Community College, Miami, FL)

Geri Creamer
(Stockton School for Adults, Stockton, CA)

Irene Dennis
(San Antonio College, San Antonio, TX)

Eileen Duffell
(P.S. 64, New York, NY)

Nancy Dunlap
(Northside Independent School District, San Antonio, TX)

Gloria Eriksson
(Old Marshall Adult Education Center, Sacramento, CA)

Judy Finkelstein
(Reseda Community Adult School, Reseda, CA)

Lawrence Fish
(Shorefront YM-YWHA English Language Program, Brooklyn, NY)

Victoria Florit
(Miami-Dade Community College, Miami, FL)

Kathleen Flynn
(Glendale Community College, Glendale, CA)

Rhoda Gilbert
(New York City Board of Education, New York, NY)

Kathleen Jimenez
(Miami-Dade Community College, Miami, FL)

Nancy Jordan
(John Jay High School Adult Education, San Antonio, TX)

Renee Klosz
(Lindsey Hopkins Technical Education Center, Miami, FL)

David Lauter
(Stockton School for Adults, Stockton, CA)

Patricia Long
(Old Marshall Adult Education Center, Sacramento, CA)

Maria Miranda
(Lindsey Hopkins Technical Education Center, Miami, FL)

Karen Moore
(Stockton School for Adults, Stockton, CA)

Erin Nyhan
(Triton College, Chicago, IL)

Marta Pitt
(Lindsey Hopkins Technical Education Center, Miami, FL)

Sylvia Rambach
(Stockton School for Adults, Stockton, CA)

Myra Redman
(Miami Dade Community College, Miami, FL)

Charleen Richardson
(San Antonio College, San Antonio, TX)

Eric Rosenbaum
(Bronx Community College, New York, NY)

Laura Rowley
(Old Marshall Adult Education Center, Sacramento, CA)

Sr. M. B. Theresa Spittle
(Stockton School for Adults, Stockton, CA)

Andre Sutton
(Belmont Adult School, Los Angeles, CA)

Jennifer Swoyer
(Northside Independent School District, San Antonio, TX)

Claire Valier
(Palm Beach County School District, West Palm Beach, FL)

The authors would like to thank Joel and Rosanne for believing in us, Eric for seeing our vision, Nancy and Sherrise for going to bat for us, and Jim, Ingrid, and Sarah for making the book a reality.

ABOUT THE AUTHORS

Rob Jenkins

I love teaching. I love to see the expressions on my students' faces when the light goes on and their eyes show such sincere joy of learning. I knew the first time I stepped into an ESL classroom that this was where I needed to be and I have never questioned that resolution. I have worked in business, sales, and publishing, and I've found challenges in all, but nothing can compare to the satisfaction of reaching people in such a personal way.

Thanks to my family who have put up with late hours and early mornings, my friends at church who support me, and all the people at Santa Anna College, School of Continuing Education who believe in me and are a source of tremendous inspiration.

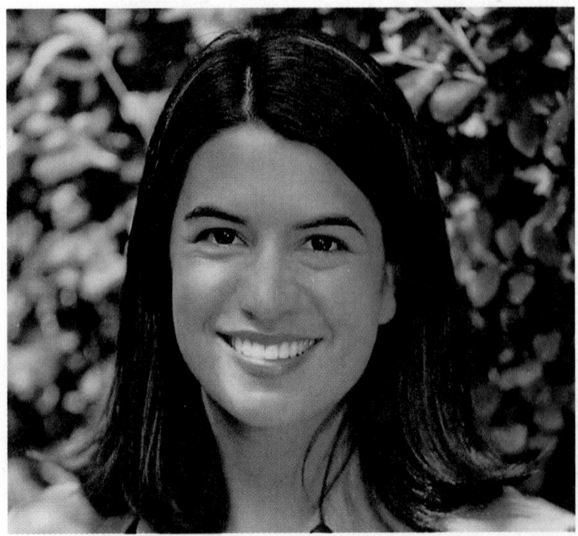

Staci Lyn Sabbagh

Ever since I can remember, I've been fascinated with other cultures and languages. I love to travel and every place I go, the first thing I want to do is meet the people, learn their language, and understand their culture. Becoming an ESL teacher was a perfect way to turn what I love to do into my profession. There's nothing more incredible than the exchange of teaching and learning from one another that goes on in an ESL classroom. And there's nothing more rewarding than helping a student succeed.

I would especially like to thank Mom, Dad, CJ, Tete, Eric, my close friends and my Santa Anna College, School of Continuing Education family. Your love and support inspired me to do something I never imagined I could. And Rob, thank you for trusting me to be part of such an amazing project.

We are lesson plan enthusiasts! We have learned that good lesson planning makes for effective teaching and, more importantly, good learning. We also believe that learning is stimulated by task-oriented activities in which students find themselves critically laboring over decisions and negotiating meaning from their own personal perspectives.

The need to write **Stand Out** came to us as we were leading a series of teacher workshops on project-based simulations designed to help students apply what they have learned. We began to teach lesson planning within our workshops in order to help teachers see how they could incorporate the activities more effectively. Even though teachers showed great interest in both the projects and planning, they often complained that lesson planning took too much time that they simply didn't have. Another obstacle was that the books available to the instructors were not conducive to planning lessons.

We decided to write our own materials by first writing lesson plans that met specific student-performance objectives. Then we developed the student pages that were needed to make the lesson plans work in the classroom. The student book only came together after the plans! Writing over 300 lesson plans has been a tremendous challenge and has helped us evaluate our own teaching and approach. It is our hope that others will discover the benefits of always following a plan in the classroom and incorporating the strategies we have included in these materials.

TO THE TEACHER

ABOUT THE SERIES

The **Stand Out** series is designed to facilitate *active* learning while challenging students to build a nurturing and effective learning community.

The student books are divided into eight distinct units, mirroring competency areas most useful to newcomers. These areas are outlined in CASAS assessment programs and different state model standards for adults. Each unit is then divided into eight lessons and a team project activity. Lessons are driven by performance objectives and are filled with challenging activities that progress from teacher-presented to student-centered tasks.

SUPPLEMENTAL MATERIALS

- The *Stand Out Lesson Planner* is in full color with 77 complete lesson plans, taking the instructor through each stage of a lesson from warm-up and review through application.
- The *Activity Bank CD-ROM* has an abundance of materials, some of which are customizable. Print or download and modify what you need for your particular class.
- The *Stand Out Grammar Challenge* is a workbook that gives additional grammar explanation and practice.
- The *Stand Out* ExamView® Pro *Test Bank CD-ROM* allows you to customize pre- and posttests for each unit as well as a pre- and posttest for the book.
- The listening scripts are found in the back of the student book and the Lesson Planner. Cassette tapes and CD-ROMs are available with focused listening activities described in the Lesson Planner.

STAND OUT LESSON PLANNER

The *Stand Out Lesson Planner* is a new and innovative approach. As many seasoned teachers know, good lesson planning can make a substantial difference in the classroom. Students continue coming to class, understanding, applying, and remembering more of what they learn. They are more confident in their learning when good lesson planning techniques are incorporated.

We have developed lesson plans that are designed to be used each day and to reduce preparation time. The planner includes:

- Standard lesson progression (Warm-up and Review, Introduction, Presentation, Practice, Evaluation, and Application)
- A creative and complete way to approach varied class lengths so that each lesson will work within a class period.
- 231 hours of classroom activities
- Time suggestions for each activity
- Pedagogical comments
- Space for teacher notes and future planning
- Identification of SCANS, EFF, and CASAS standards

USER QUESTIONS ABOUT STAND OUT

- **What are SCANS and EFF and how do they integrate into the book?**
  SCANS is the **S**ecretary's **C**ommission on **A**cquiring **N**ecessary **S**kills. SCANS was developed to encourage students to prepare for the workplace. The standards developed through SCANS have been incorporated throughout the **Stand Out** student books and components.

  Stand Out addresses SCANS a little differently than other books. SCANS standards elicit effective teaching strategies by incorporating essential skills such as critical thinking and group work. We have incorporated SCANS standards in every lesson, not isolating these standards in the work unit, as is typically done.

  EFF, or **E**quipped **f**or the **F**uture, is another set of standards established to address students' roles as parents, workers, and citizens, with a vision of student literacy and lifelong learning. **Stand Out** addresses these standards and integrates them into the materials in a similar way to SCANS.

- **What about CASAS?** The federal government has mandated that states show student outcomes as a prerequisite to funding. Some states have incorporated the **C**omprehensive **A**dult **S**tudent **A**ssessment **S**ystem (CASAS) testing to standardize agency reporting. Unfortunately, since many of our students are unfamiliar with standardized testing and therefore struggle with it, adult schools need to develop lesson plans to address specific concerns. **Stand Out** was developed with careful attention to CASAS skill areas in most lessons and performance objectives.

- **Are the tasks too challenging for my students?** Students learn by doing and learn more when challenged. **Stand Out** provides tasks that encourage critical thinking in a variety of ways. The tasks in each lesson move from teacher-directed to student-centered so the learner clearly understands what's expected and is willing to "take a risk." The lessons are expected to be challenging. In this way, students learn that when they work together as a learning community, anything becomes possible. The satisfaction of accomplishing something both as an individual and as a member of a team results in greater confidence and effective learning.

- **Do I need to understand lesson planning to teach from the student book?** If you don't understand lesson planning when you start, you will when you finish! Teaching from **Stand Out** is like a course on lesson planning, especially if you use the Lesson Planner on a daily basis.

  Stand Out does *stand out* because, when we developed this series, we first established performance objectives for each lesson. Then we designed lesson plans, followed by student book pages. The introduction to each lesson varies because different objectives demand different approaches. **Stand Out's** variety of tasks makes learning more interesting for the student.

- **What are team projects?** The final lesson of each unit is a **team project.** This is often a team simulation that incorporates the objectives of the unit and provides an additional opportunity for students to actively apply what they have learned. The project allows students to produce something that represents their progress in learning. These end-of-unit projects were created with a variety of learning styles and individual skills in mind. The team projects can be skipped or simplified, but we encourage instructors to implement them, enriching the overall student experience.

- **What do you mean by a customizable Activity Bank?** Every class, student, teacher, and approach is different. Since no one textbook can meet all these differences, the *Activity Bank CD-ROM* allows you to customize **Stand Out** for your class. You can copy different activities and worksheets from the CD-ROM to your hard drive and then:

  - change items in supplemental vocabulary, grammar, and life skill activities;
  - personalize activities with student names and popular locations in your area;
  - extend every lesson with additional practice where you feel it is most needed.

- **Is this a grammar-based or a competency-based series?** This is a competency-based series, with grammar identified more clearly and more boldly than in other similar series. We believe that grammar instruction in context is extremely important. Grammar structures are frequently identified as principal lesson objectives. Students are first provided with context that incorporates the grammar, followed by an explanation and practice. The students are exposed to grammar in context that will help them acquire the structures in later levels. For teachers who want to enhance grammar instruction, the *Activity Bank CD-ROM* and/or the *Stand Out Grammar Challenge* workbooks provide ample opportunities.

  The six competencies that drive **Stand Out** are basic communication, consumer economics, community resources, health, occupational knowledge, and lifelong learning (government and law replace lifelong learning in Books 3 and 4).

- **Are there enough activities so I don't have to supplement? Stand Out** stands alone in providing 231 hours of instruction and activities, even without the additional suggestions in the Lesson Planner. The Lesson Planner also shows you how to streamline lessons to provide 115 hours of classwork and still have thorough lessons if you meet less often. When supplementing with the Activity Bank CD-ROM, the ExamView Test Bank CD-ROM, and the Stand Out Grammar Challenge workbooks, you gain unlimited opportunities to extend class hours and provide activities related directly to each lesson objective. Calculate how many hours your class meets in a semester and look to **Stand Out** to address the full class experience.

  Stand Out is a comprehensive approach to adult language learning, meeting needs of students and instructors completely and effectively.

CONTENTS

◆ Grammar points that are explicitly taught. ❖ Grammar points that are presented in context.

EFF	SCANS (Workplace)	Math	CASAS
• Speaking so others can understand • Listening actively	• Listening • Speaking • Sociability	• Understand and write numerals 0–20	**1:** 0.1.1, 0.1.4, 0.2.1 **2:** 0.2.1, 0.1.6 **3:** 0.1.5, 0.2.1 **4:** 0.1.2, 0.1.5, 0.1.6
Most EFF skills are incorporated into this unit, with an emphasis on: • Conveying ideas in writing • Taking responsibility for learning • Reflecting and evaluating (Technology is optional.)	Most SCANS are incorporated into this unit, with an emphasis on: • Acquiring information • Interpreting and evaluating information • Writing (Technology is optional.)	• Use units of measurement: feet, inches, pounds • State dates: day, month, and year • Tell time: hour, half hour, and quarter hour • Write times of the day in numerals	**1:** 0.1.6, 0.2.1, 1.1.3, 2.7.2, 6.7.2 **2:** 0.1.4, 0.2.1 **3:** 0.1.2, 0.2.1, 0.2.2 **4:** 0.1.2 **5:** 0.1.2 **6:** 0.1.2, 0.2.1, 0.2.4 **7:** 0.1.2, 0.1.5, 0.2.1 **R:** 7.1.1, 7.1.4, 7.4.1, 7.4.9, 7.4.10, 7.5.1 **TP:** 4.8.1, 4.8.5
Most EFF skills are incorporated into this unit, with an emphasis on: • Using mathematics in problem solving and communication • Solving problems and making decisions • Reflecting and evaluating (Technology is optional.)	Most SCANS are incorporated into this unit, with an emphasis on: • Allocating money • Serving customers • Organizing and maintaining information • Decision making (Technology is optional.)	• Interpret data on a bar graph • Create a bar graph • Use addition and multiplication to calculate totals • Count U.S. currency • Understand and write prices • Write a check	**1:** 1.3.8, 1.3.9, 4.8.1 **2:** 1.1.6, 1.3.9, 1.6.4 **3:** 1.2.1, 1.3.1, 1.3.9 **4:** 0.1.2, 1.3.9 **5:** 1.3.9, 7.2.3 **6:** 1.3.1, 1.8.2 **7:** 0.1.2, 1.2.2, 1.2.4 **R:** 7.1.1, 7.1.4, 7.4.1, 7.4.9 **TP:** 4.6.1, 4.8.1, 4.8.5
Most EFF skills are incorporated into this unit, with an emphasis on: • Using mathematics in problem solving and communication • Learning through research (Technology is optional.)	Most SCANS are incorporated into this unit, with an emphasis on: • Allocating money • Understanding systems • Creative thinking • Seeing things in the mind's eye (Technology is optional.)	• Interpret and create a bar graph • Use addition to calculate totals • Understand U.S. units of measurement: *pounds, ounces, gallons, pints* • Interpret measurements in recipes • Compare prices per pound and per unit • Compare prices and calculate savings	**1:** 1.1.3, 1.3.8, 6.7.2 **2:** 1.3.6, 1.3.8, 2.2.1, 6.1.1 **3:** 1.3.8, 2.6.4 **4:** 1.1.7, 1.2.1, 1.3.8 **5:** 1.2.1 **6:** 1.1.7, 1.2.1, 1.2.2, 1.2.4 **7:** 1.1.1, 1.1.4 **R:** 7.1.1, 7.1.4, 7.4.1, 7.4.9 **TP:** 4.6.1, 4.8.1, 4.8.5, 6.1.1
Most EFF skills are incorporated into this unit, with an emphasis on: • Solving problems and making decisions • Planning • Reflecting and evaluating (Technology is optional.)	Most SCANS are incorporated into this unit, with an emphasis on: • Acquiring and evaluating information • Creative thinking • Seeing things in the mind's eye (Technology is optional.)	• Interpret and create a pie chart • Compare rents of apartments and houses • Interpret categories in a family budget • Make a budget plan • Use addition and subtraction to calculate expenses and savings	**1:** 1.4.1, 6.7.4 **2:** 1.4.1 **3:** 1.4.1, 1.4.2 **4:** 1.4.2 **5:** 4.6.1 **6:** 1.5.1, 6.1.1 **7:** 1.5.1, 1.5.2 **R:** 7.1.1, 7.1.4, 7.4.1, 7.4.9, 7.4.10, 7.5.1 **TP:** 4.8.1, 4.8.5

CASAS: Numbers in bold indicate lesson numbers; **R** indicates review lesson; **TP** indicates team project.

CONTENTS

◆ Grammar points that are explicitly taught. ❖ Grammar points that are presented in context.

EFF	SCANS (Workplace)	MATH	CASAS
Most EFF skills are incorporated into this unit, with an emphasis on: • Reading with understanding • Solving problems and making decisions • Learning through research (Technology is optional.)	Most SCANS are incorporated into this unit, with an emphasis on: • Acquiring and evaluating information • Reading • Seeing things in the mind's eye • Sociability (Technology is optional.)	• Interpret spatial relationships: *in, on, between, next to, across from, in the corner* • Understand phone numbers • Create a bar graph	**1:** 2.5.1 **2:** 1.1.3, 1.9.4, 2.2.1, 2.2.5 **3:** 1.1.3, 1.9.4, 2.2.1, 2.2.5, 2.5.4 **4:** 1.1.3, 1.3.7, 2.5.4 **5:** 2.1.1, 2.5.1, 2.5.2, 2.5.3 **6:** 2.1.7, 2.1.8 **7:** 0.2.3 **R:** 7.1.1, 7.1.4, 7.4.1, 7.4.9, 7.4.10, 7.5.1 **TP:** 4.8.1, 4.8.5
Most EFF skills are incorporated into this unit, with an emphasis on: • Solving problems and making decisions • Reflecting and evaluating • Learning through research (Technology is optional.)	Most SCANS are incorporated into this unit, with an emphasis on: • Interpreting and communicating information • Understanding systems • Decision making (Technology is optional.)	• Interpret data in a Venn diagram • Complete a Venn diagram • Determine temperatures on a thermometer using Celsius and Fahrenheit	**1:** 3.1.1 **2:** 1.1.5, 3.1.1 **3:** 3.1.1, 3.3.1 **4:** 3.3.1, 3.3.2, 3.4.1 **5:** 0.1.6, 2.1.2 **6:** 2.2.1, 2.5.1, 2.5.4 **7:** 3.5.9 **R:** 7.1.1, 7.1.4, 7.4.1, 7.4.9, 7.4.10, 7.5.1 **TP:** 4.8.1, 4.8.5
Most EFF skills are incorporated into this unit, with an emphasis on: • Solving problems and making decisions • Learning through research (Technology is optional.)	Most SCANS are incorporated into this unit, with an emphasis on: • Organizing and maintaining information • Understanding systems • Creative thinking • Decision making (Technology is optional.)	• Interpret and compare information about wages • Interpret data including dates in an employment application	**1:** 4.1.8, 4.8.1 **2:** 4.1.3, 4.1.6, 4.1.8 **3:** 4.1.8, 4.1.2 **4:** 4.1.5, 4.1.7 **5:** 4.1.2, 4.1.8, 4.5.1 **6:** 4.3.1 **7:** 4.4.1, 4.4.4 **R:** 7.1.1, 7.1.4, 7.4.1, 7.4.9, 7.4.10, 7.5.1 **TP:** 4.8.1, 4.8.2, 4.8.5
Most EFF skills are incorporated into this unit, with an emphasis on: • Planning • Taking responsibility for learning • Reflecting and evaluating (Technology is optional.)	Most SCANS are incorporated into this unit, with an emphasis on: • Understanding systems • Monitoring and correcting performance • Knowing how to learn • Self-management (Technology is optional.)	• Tell time • Use multiplication and addition to calculate totals • Estimate time spent on different activities • Use ordinal numbers	**1:** 6.7.2, 7.1.1, 7.3.1, 7.3.2, 7.4.1 **2:** 7.1.4, 7.4.1, 7.4.3 **3:** 2.3.1, 6.6.6, 7.1.1, 7.1.4, 7.4.1 **4:** 7.1.1, 7.1.4, 7.2.3 **5:** 7.11, 7.2.6 **6:** 7.1.1, 7.5.1 **7:** 7.1.4, 7.4.1 **R:** 7.1.1, 7.1.3, 7.1.4, 7.4.1, 7.4.9, 7.5.10, 7.5.1 **TP:** 7.1.1, 7.1.2, 7.1.3, 7.1.4, 7.4.1

CASAS: Numbers in bold indicate lesson numbers; **R** indicates review lesson; **TP** indicates team project.

Guide to Stand Out

Meeting the Standards has never been easier!

Stand Out is an easy-to-use, standards-based series for adult students that teaches the English skills necessary to be a successful worker, parent, and citizen.

- **Goals:** A roadmap of learning is provided for the student.
- **Vocabulary:** Key vocabulary is introduced visually and aurally.

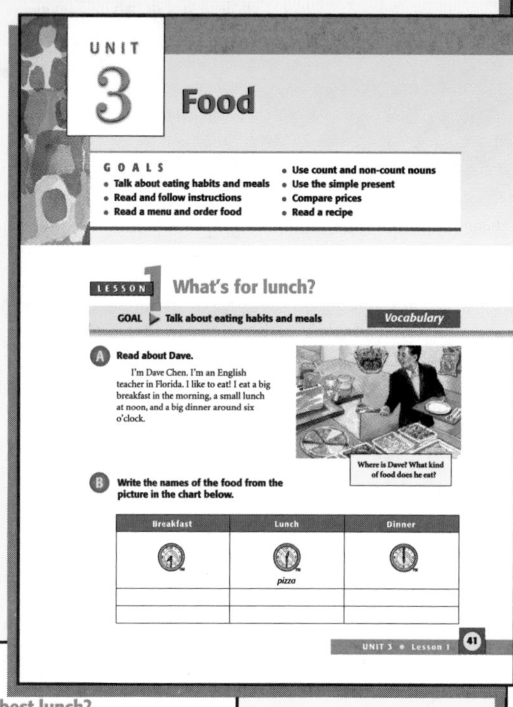

UNIT 3 Food

GOALS
- Talk about eating habits and meals
- Read and follow instructions
- Read a menu and order food
- Use count and non-count nouns
- Use the simple present
- Compare prices
- Read a recipe

LESSON 1 What's for lunch?

GOAL ▶ Talk about eating habits and meals — Vocabulary

A Read about Dave.

I'm Dave Chen. I'm an English teacher in Florida. I like to eat! I eat a big breakfast in the morning, a small lunch at noon, and a big dinner around six o'clock.

Where is Dave? What kind of food does he eat?

B Write the names of the food from the picture in the chart below.

Breakfast	Lunch	Dinner
	pizza	

UNIT 3 • Lesson 1 41

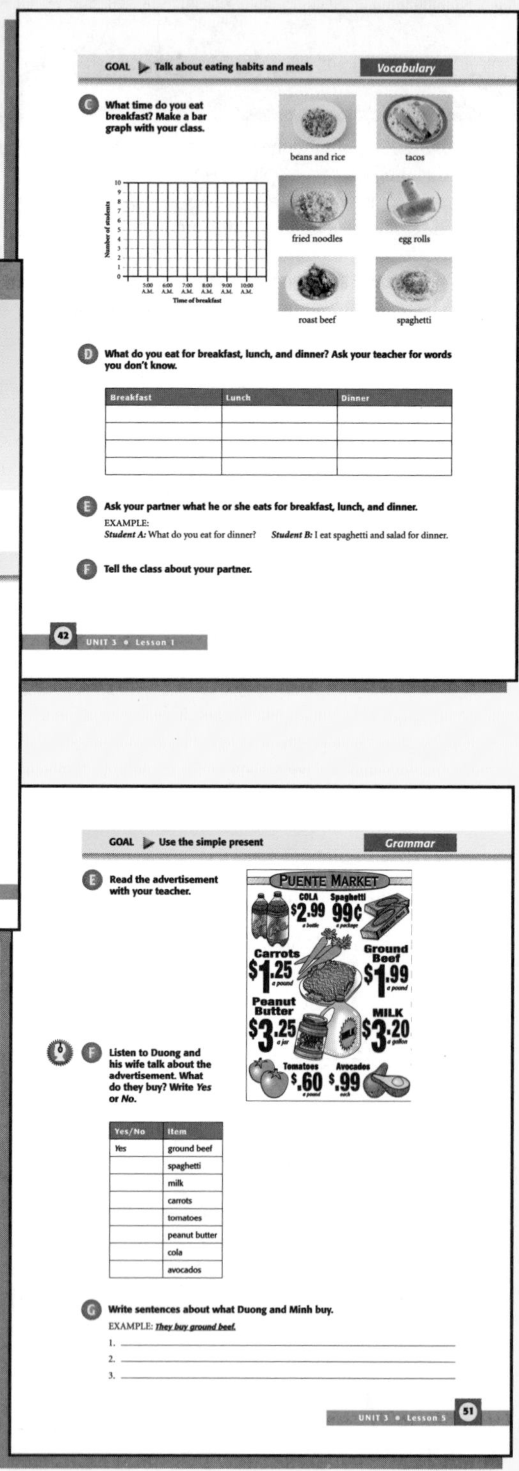

GOAL ▶ Talk about eating habits and meals — Vocabulary

C What time do you eat breakfast? Make a bar graph with your class.

D What do you eat for breakfast, lunch, and dinner? Ask your teacher for words you don't know.

Breakfast	Lunch	Dinner

E Ask your partner what he or she eats for breakfast, lunch, and dinner.

EXAMPLE:
Student A: What do you eat for dinner? *Student B:* I eat spaghetti and salad for dinner.

F Tell the class about your partner.

42 UNIT 3 • Lesson 1

GOAL ▶ Use the simple present — Grammar

E Read the advertisement with your teacher.

PUENTE MARKET
COLA $2.99
Spaghetti 99¢
Carrots $1.25
Ground Beef $1.99
Peanut Butter $3.25
MILK $3.20
Tomatoes $.60
Avocados $.99

F Listen to Duong and his wife talk about the advertisement. What do they buy? Write *Yes* or *No*.

Yes/No	Item
Yes	ground beef
	spaghetti
	milk
	carrots
	tomatoes
	peanut butter
	cola
	avocados

G Write sentences about what Duong and Minh buy.

EXAMPLE: *They buy ground beef.*

1. ___
2. ___
3. ___

UNIT 3 • Lesson 5 51

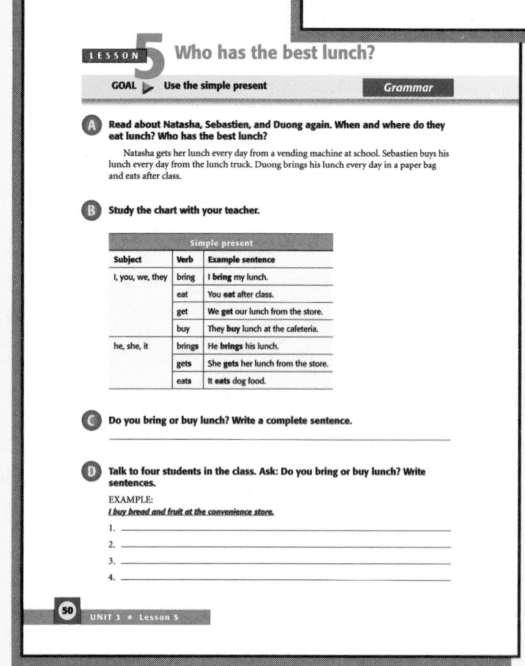

LESSON 5 Who has the best lunch?

GOAL ▶ Use the simple present — Grammar

A Read about Natasha, Sebastien, and Duong again. When and where do they eat lunch? Who has the best lunch?

Natasha gets her lunch every day from a vending machine at school. Sebastien buys his lunch every day from the lunch truck. Duong brings his lunch every day in a paper bag and eats after class.

B Study the chart with your teacher.

Simple present		
Subject	Verb	Example sentence
I, you, we, they	bring	I **bring** my lunch.
	eat	You **eat** after class.
	get	We **get** our lunch from the store.
	buy	They **buy** lunch at the cafeteria.
he, she, it	brings	He **brings** his lunch.
	gets	She **gets** her lunch from the store.
	eats	It **eats** dog food.

C Do you bring or buy lunch? Write a complete sentence.

D Talk to four students in the class. Ask: Do you bring or buy lunch? Write sentences.

EXAMPLE:
I buy bread and fruit at the convenience store.

1. ___
2. ___
3. ___
4. ___

50 UNIT 3 • Lesson 5

- **Grammar:** Clear explanations are followed by immediate use, in this example, with reading and writing.
- **Grammar:** Charts clearly explain grammar points, and are followed by controlled exercises leading into open-ended ones.

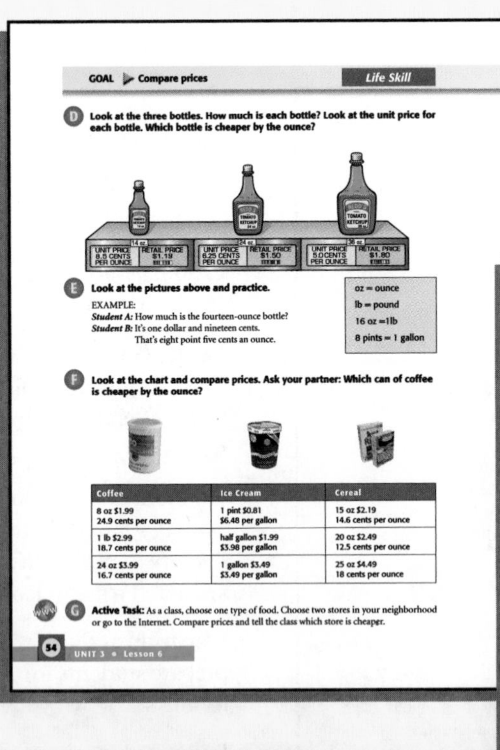

GOAL ▶ Compare prices — Life Skill

D **Look at the three bottles. How much is each bottle? Look at the unit price for each bottle. Which bottle is cheaper by the ounce?**

E **Look at the pictures above and practice.**

EXAMPLE:
Student A: How much is the fourteen-ounce bottle?
Student B: It's one dollar and nineteen cents. That's eight point five cents an ounce.

oz = ounce
lb = pound
16 oz = 1 lb
8 pints = 1 gallon

F **Look at the chart and compare prices. Ask your partner: Which can of coffee is cheaper by the ounce?**

Coffee	Ice Cream	Cereal
8 oz $1.99 24.9 cents per ounce	1 pint $0.81 $6.48 per gallon	15 oz $2.19 14.6 cents per ounce
1 lb $2.99 18.7 cents per ounce	half gallon $1.99 $3.98 per gallon	20 oz $2.49 12.5 cents per ounce
24 oz $3.99 16.7 cents per ounce	1 gallon $3.49 $3.49 per gallon	25 oz $4.49 18 cents per ounce

G **Active Task:** As a class, choose one type of food. Choose two stores in your neighborhood or go to the Internet. Compare prices and tell the class which store is cheaper.

54 UNIT 3 • Lesson 6

- **Life Skills:** State- and federally-required life skills and competencies (i.e. EFF, CASAS, SCANS, Model Standards, etc.) help students meet necessary benchmarks.
- **Math Skills:** Contextualized math activities are integrated throughout.

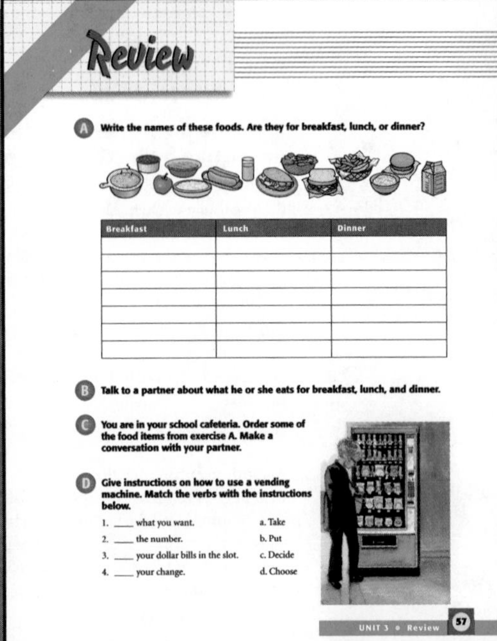

Review

A **Write the names of these foods. Are they for breakfast, lunch, or dinner?**

Breakfast	Lunch	Dinner

B **Talk to a partner about what he or she eats for breakfast, lunch, and dinner.**

C **You are in your school cafeteria. Order some of the food items from exercise A. Make a conversation with your partner.**

D **Give instructions on how to use a vending machine. Match the verbs with the instructions below.**

1. ____ what you want. a. Take
2. ____ the number. b. Put
3. ____ your dollar bills in the slot. c. Decide
4. ____ your change. d. Choose

UNIT 3 • Review 57

- **Review:** A summary of key grammar, vocabulary, and life skills; it gives students an opportunity to synthesize what they have learned.

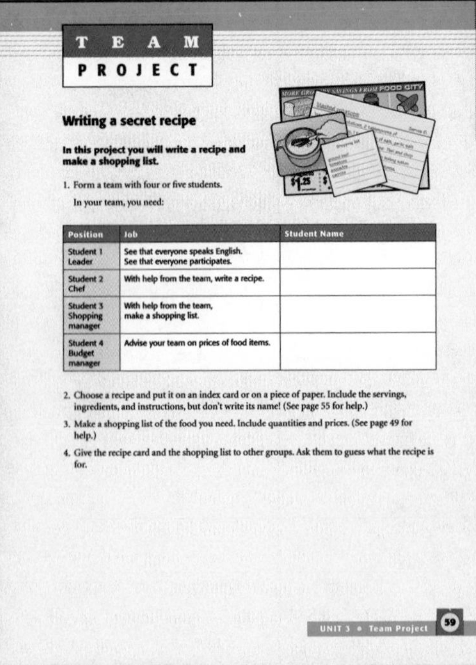

TEAM PROJECT

Writing a secret recipe

In this project you will write a recipe and make a shopping list.

1. Form a team with four or five students.

   In your team, you need:

Position	Job	Student Name
Student 1 Leader	See that everyone speaks English. See that everyone participates.	
Student 2 Chef	With help from the team, write a recipe.	
Student 3 Shopping manager	With help from the team, make a shopping list.	
Student 4 Budget manager	Advise your team on prices of food items.	

2. Choose a recipe and put it on an index card or on a piece of paper. Include the servings, ingredients, and instructions, but don't write its name! (See page 55 for help.)
3. Make a shopping list of the food you need. Include quantities and prices. (See page 49 for help.)
4. Give the recipe card and the shopping list to other groups. Ask them to guess what the recipe is for.

UNIT 3 • Team Project 59

- **Team Projects:** Project-based activities utilize SCANS competencies (e.g., making decisions, working on a team, developing interpersonal skills, etc.) and provide motivation for students.

PRONUNCIATION

Can you hear the sounds /j/ and /y/ in these words? Listen and repeat.

jar	jelly	juice	package	orange	margarine
yes	yogurt	use	mayonnaise	menu	papaya

LEARNER LOG

Circle what you learned and write the page number where you learned it.

1. I can talk about meals and food.
   Yes Maybe No Page ______
2. I can use a vending machine.
   Yes Maybe No Page ______
3. I can read a menu.
   Yes Maybe No Page ______
4. I can place an order.
   Yes Maybe No Page ______
5. I can read an advertisement.
   Yes Maybe No Page ______
6. I can use count and non-count nouns.
   Yes Maybe No Page ______
7. I can comparison shop.
   Yes Maybe No Page ______
8. I can read a recipe.
   Yes Maybe No Page ______

Did you answer *No* to any questions? Review the information with a partner.

Rank what you like to do best from 1 to 6. 1 is your favorite activity. Your teacher will help you.

- ☐ practice listening
- ☐ practice speaking
- ☐ practice reading
- ☐ practice writing
- ☐ learn new words (vocabulary)
- ☐ learn grammar

In the next unit I want to practice more ______________.

60 UNIT 3 • Pronunciation and Learner Log

- **Pronunciation:** Specific pronunciation problems are targeted and corrected.
- **Learner Log:** The final section of each unit provides opportunity for learner self-assessment.

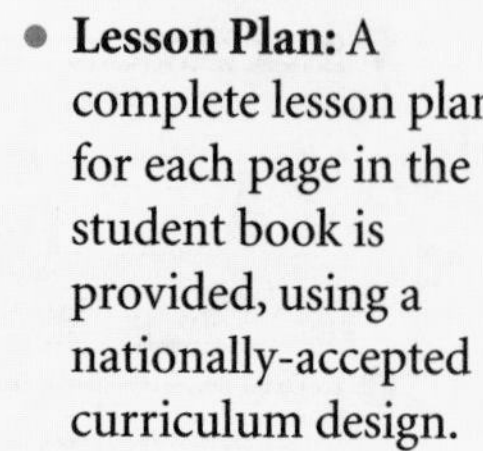

LESSON PLAN

Objective:
Identify eating habits and meals
Key vocabulary:
eggs, toast, orange juice, pizza, salad, potato chips, apples, corn, chicken, tea, rice, vegetables, size, meal, noodles, eggrolls, spaghetti, roast beef, tacos, healthy, hot, cold, breakfast, lunch, dinner

TB

Pre-Assessment: Use the *Stand Out* ExamView® Pro *Test Bank* for Unit 3. *(optional)*

Warm-up and Review: 10–20 min. 1.5+

Write the word *favorite* on the board. Tell the students what your favorite meal is. Write the words ***breakfast***, ***lunch***, and ***dinner*** on the board and above them write ***meals***. Ask the students what their favorite meal is and take a class poll.

Introduction: 1 min. 1.5+

State objective: ***Today and in this unit you will learn about food and eating habits.***

Presentation 1: 15–20 min. 1.5+

Ask students to open to this page and talk about the picture of Dave. Ask the questions in the box and any additional ones that you consider appropriate. See how much vocabulary the students know by asking them to identify the foods in the picture. Make a list of the foods on the board and help them with those they don't know.

A Read about Dave.

Do the reading as a class. Review the meal vocabulary the students learned in the Warm-up and Review.

Practice 1: 10–15 min. 1.5+

B Write the names of the food from the picture in the chart below.

Ask the students in pairs or in groups to classify the vocabulary. Then ask the pairs or groups to get together with other pairs or groups to see if they have classified the foods in the same way. In different cultures, foods for meals may differ, so accept any answer.

Evaluation 1: 5–10 min. 1.5+

Discuss differences in food preferences with the class.

Pronunciation:

An optional pronunciation activity is found on the final page of this unit. This pronunciation activity may be introduced during any lesson in this unit, especially if students need practice contrasting the sounds of /j/ and /y/. Go to pages 60/60a for Unit 3 Pronunciation.

STANDARDS CORRELATIONS

CASAS: 1.1.3, 1.3.8, 6.7.2, 7.2.3, 7.2.6
SCANS: **Resources** Allocates Materials and Facility Resources
Interpersonal Participates as a Member of a Team, Teaches Others New Skills, Exercises Leadership
Information Acquires and Evaluates Information, Organizes and Maintains Information, Interprets and Communicates Information, Uses Computers to Process Information (optional)
Technology Applies Technology to Task (optional)
Basic Skills Reading, Listening, Speaking
Thinking Skills Problem Solving, Seeing Things in the Mind's Eye
EFF: **Communication** Read with Understanding, Speak So Others Can Understand, Listen Actively, Observe Critically
Decision Making Solve Problems and Make Decisions
Interpersonal Guide Others, Cooperate with Others
Lifelong Learning Use Information and Communications Technology (optional)

- **Lesson Plan:** A complete lesson plan for each page in the student book is provided, using a nationally-accepted curriculum design.
- **Pacing Guides:** Class-length icons offer three different pacing strategies.
- **CD Icon:** Supplemental activities found on the *Activity Bank CD-ROM* are noted with an icon.
- **Warm-up activities** prepare students for lessons.
- **Suggested Internet activities** expose students to technology and real world activities.

Unit 3
Worksheet 7

Name: ____________
Date: ____________

Comparison Shopping

A. Study the chart.

Salad Dressing			Tomato Sauce			Milk			Cereal		
ounces	price	cents per ounce	ounces	price	cents per ounce	Size	price	cents per ounce	ounces	price	cents per ounce
8	$ 1.99	24.9	8	$ .25	3.2	pint	$ .81	5.1	15	$ 2.19	14.6
16	$ 2.99	18.7	15	$ .75	5.0	half gallon	$ 1.99	3.2	20	$ 2.49	12.5
24	$ 3.99	16.7	28	$ 1.29	4.5	gallon	$ 3.49	2.7	25	$ 4.49	18.0

B. In a group, and with the teacher, answer the questions about the chart.

1. What is the price of a pint of milk? ______
2. What is the cost per ounce for a 16-ounce bottle of salad dressing? ______
3. What is the price for a 25-ounce box of cereal? ______
4. What's cheaper by the ounce, a half-gallon of milk or a gallon of milk?
5. Is $.75 for a 15-ounce can of tomato sauce a good price?

C. In a group, write what you think are good prices and not very good prices.

Good prices	Not very good prices
24-ounce can of salad dressing	

Heinle & Heinle © 2002
Stand Out 1 Activity Bank

Imperatives

UNIT 3 **Food**

CHALLENGE 6 ▸ Imperatives

Use imperatives...	Affirmative	Negative
to give instructions	**Choose** a number.	**Don't boil** the potatoes.
to make a request (Add **please** to be polite.)	**Buy** milk, please.	**Don't eat** in the library, please.
to make a command	**Eat** your vegetables.	**Don't put** your feet on the tables.

• When we use the imperative, we understand the subject is **you**.

A **Choose a verb from the box to complete the sentences. Use the negative form when indicated. More than one answer is possible for some sentences.**

read	listen	ask	don't put
help	write	don't use	don't eat
don't take	don't cook	cut	

EXAMPLE: ***Help*** ______ your sister make dinner.

1. ______ the server about the menu.
2. ______ the shopping list.
3. ______ my bowl.
4. ______ to your parents.
5. ______ eggs in the microwave.
6. ______ candy all day.
7. ______ the carrots into half.
8. ______ a check for the food.
9. ______ the dog to the restaurant.
10. ______ pennies in the vending machine.

B **Silvia is getting ready for a party. Read the instructions she gives her children. Fill in the imperative. Use the negative form when indicated.**

EXAMPLE: ***Don't watch*** ______ (watch, negative) TV now.

I need your help. Please ______ (1. vacuum) the rug and ______ (2. clean) your rooms. ______ (3. eat, negative) the snacks in the living room. ______ (4. buy) eggs, milk, and bread. ______ (5. buy, negative) the food at the convenience store. ______ (6. go) to Food City. ______ (7. peel) and ______ (8. whip) the potatoes. ______ (9. make) a salad. ______ (10. wash) and ______ (11. drain) the lettuce first. Then ______ (12. set) the table. ______ (13. use, negative) the blue plates. Use the white plates. ______ (14. choose) some pretty napkins. ______ (15. put) on some nice clothes.

22 UNIT 3

- *Activity Bank CD-ROM:* Hours of motivating and creative reinforcement activities are provided to follow student book lessons. Instructors can download activities and add or adapt them to student needs. The audio component for listening activities will also be on CD-ROMs. Cassettes are available for instructors who prefer them.

Pre-Test Unit 3

A. Read the prices. Then choose the correct total for each shopping list below.

Sam's Food Mart		24-7 Convenience Store		Farmer's Market	
Tomato Sauce	$1.20	Bread	$1.65	Cucumbers (each)	$1.00
Milk	$1.10	Peanut butter	$2.35	Apples (per bag)	$1.50
Cereal	$2.40	Potato chips	$2.70		

1. Tomato sauce, cereal, milk.

   a. $5.60 b. $5.70 c. $4.70 d. $3.60

2. Milk, bread, apples.

   a. $3.55 b. $4.15 c. $4.25 d. $4.05

3. Potato chips, 2 cucumbers, 1 bag of apples.

   a. $6.20 b. $5.20 c. $6.70 d. $5.50

B. Match the food with the correct container.

____1. can	a. cheese
____2. box	b. soup
____3. package	c. water
____4. bottle	d. potato chips
____5. jar	e. cookies
____6. bag	f. jelly

- *Stand Out Grammar Challenge:* Optional workbook activities provide supplemental exercises for students who desire even more contextual grammar and vocabulary practice.

- *Stand Out* ExamView®Pro *Test Bank:* Innovative test bank CD-ROM allows for pre-and post-unit quizzes. Teachers can easily print out predetermined tests, or modify them to create their own customized (including computer-based) assessments.

PRE-UNIT

Welcome to Our Class

GOALS

- Greet your friends
- Spell aloud
- Say and understand numbers
- Understand classroom instructions

LESSON 1 Hello!

GOAL ▶ **Greet your friends** *Life Skill*

LESSON 2 Spell your name

GOAL ▶ **Spell aloud** | ***Life Skill***

Listen and repeat.

Hi! I'm Gabriela.
G–A–B–R–I–E–L–A

Hello! I'm Duong.
D–U–O–N–G

B Practice spelling aloud. Listen and repeat.

Aa	Bb	Cc	Dd	Ee	Ff	Gg
Hh	Ii	Jj	Kk	Ll	Mm	Nn
Oo	Pp	Qq	Rr	Ss	Tt	Uu
Vv	Ww	Xx	Yy	Zz		

C Listen and write.

1. Hi! I'm ____________________.
2. Hello! My name's ____________________.
3. How are you? I'm ____________________.
4. Hi! My name's ____________________.

D Spell your name to your partner. Listen and write your partner's name.

____

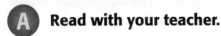

LESSON 3 Numbers

GOAL ▶ Say and understand numbers **Life Skill**

A **Read with your teacher.**

There are 12 students in our class. We study English for 6 hours every week. Our school address is 19 Lincoln Street, Los Angeles. The zip code is 78014.

B **Listen and practice saying the numbers 0 to 20.**

0	1	2	3	4	5	6	7	8	9	10
11	12	13	14	15	16	17	18	19	20	

C **Listen and write the numbers you hear.**

a. ______________ c. ______________ e. ______________

b. ______________ d. ______________ f. ______________

D **Write these numbers. Say the numbers to your partner. Listen and write your partner's numbers.**

	You	Your partner
1. The number of people in your family.	______________	______________
2. Your phone number.	______________	______________
3. Your house number.	______________	______________
4. Your zip code.	______________	______________

E **Listen and write the missing numbers.**

My name is Gabriela. My address is ______________ Main Street. The zip code is ______________. The phone number is ____________________. There are ______________ students in my class.

LESSON 4 Classroom talk

GOAL ▶ **Understand classroom instructions** — ***Life Skill***

Write the correct word below each picture.

write	read	listen	speak

____

____

____

____

B **Use the words from the box to complete these classroom instructions.**

EXAMPLE: ***Write*** your answers on the board.

1. ______________ to the tape and repeat.
2. ______________ your answers on a piece of paper.
3. ______________ the story and answer the questions.
4. ______________ with your partner and make a new conversation.

C **Listen and follow the instructions.**

D Tell your partner.

Please stand up.
Please take out your book and open to page fifteen.
Please sit down.
Please write my name on a piece of paper.
Please read my name.

E Practice the conversation with your teacher.

Teacher: Please open your books to page fifteen.
You: What page?
Teacher: Page fifteen. That's one, five.
You: Thank you.

F Practice with a partner.

Student B's book is closed.
Student A says:

1. Please open your book to page six.
2. Please open your book to page fourteen.
3. Please open your book to page sixteen.
4. Please open your book to page eight.
5. Please open your book to page nine.
6. Please open your book to page twenty.

Student A's book is closed.
Student B says:

7. Please open your book to page three.
8. Please open your book to page twelve.
9. Please open your book to page eleven.
10. Please open your book to page four.
11. Please open your book to page seventeen.
12. Please open your book to page nineteen.

UNIT 1

Talking with Others

GOALS

- Talk about places and names
- Use *be* and introduce people
- Describe people
- Use the verb *have*
- Describe families
- Use *like* in the present tense
- Tell time

LESSON 1 What's your name?

GOAL ▶ Talk about places and names — *Life Skill*

Where is Roberto from?

A Read about Roberto.

My name is Roberto Garcia. I'm a new student in this school. I'm from Mexico City, Mexico. I'm very happy in my new class.

B Write about yourself.

My name is ______________________. I'm from ______________________.

Listen and fill in the missing information.

Names: *Roberto, Eva, Gabriela, Duong*
Countries: *Argentina, Vietnam, Poland, Mexico*

Name: ______________ Garcia
Age: 43
City: Mexico City
Country: ______________

Name: ______________ Bui
Age: 30
City: Hanoi
Country: ______________

Name: ______________ Malinska
Age: 60
City: Warsaw
Country: ______________

Name: ______________ Ramirez
Age: 26
City: Buenos Aires
Country: ______________

Make sentences about each person.

EXAMPLE: ***Roberto is 43 years old. He is from Mexico City, Mexico.***

1. ______________________________
2. ______________________________
3. ______________________________

E **Find Roberto's, Duong's, Eva's, and Gabriela's countries. Mark them with an "X".**

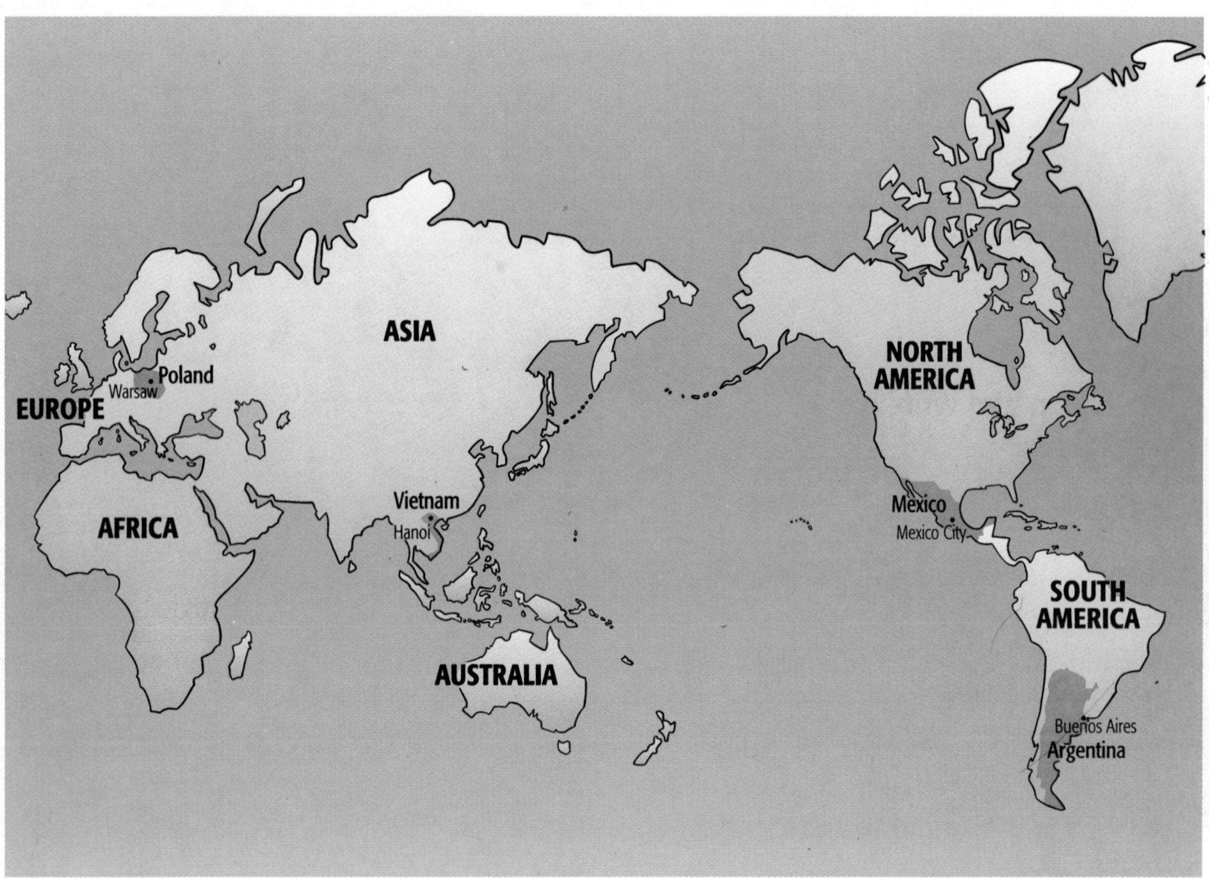

F **Practice the conversation with five students. Ask where they are from and mark the places on the map.**

EXAMPLE:
Student A: Where are you from?
Student B: I'm from Mexico City, Mexico. It's right here on the map.

G **Active Task:** Go to the library or use the Internet to find out more about your classmates' hometowns or countries.

LESSON 2

Introductions

GOAL ▶ Use *be* and introduce people

Grammar

Where are the people in the picture?
What are they saying?

A **Listen and write about Felipe.**

Name: *Felipe*

Country: ____________

Age: ____________

Marital Status: ____________

Marital Status:
single
married
divorced

B **Make groups of four. Interview three students.**

What's your name?	Where are you from?	How old are you?	Are you married or single?
Ex. *Roberto*	*Mexico*	*43 years old*	*married*
1.			
2.			
3.			

C **Listen and write.**

My name is Tatsuya. This is my new friend, Felipe. Felipe ____________ ____________ Cuba. ____________ ____________ 23 years old. He ____________ ____________. We ____________ students in this class.

D **Introduce one new friend in your group to another group. Follow the example in exercise C.**

Study the chart with your teacher.

be		
Subject	**Verb**	**Example sentence**
I	am	I am from Mexico.
you	are	You are married.
he, she, it	is	She is 30 years old.
we	are	We are friends.
they	are	They are students.

Roberto Garcia
Age: 43 years old
Marital status: Married
Country: Mexico

Duong Bui
Age: 30 years old
Marital status: Married
Country: Vietnam

Eva Malinska
Age: 60 years old
Marital status: Divorced
Country: Poland

Felipe Rodriguez
Age: 23 years old
Marital status: Single
Country: Cuba

Nam Nguyen
Age: 58 years old
Marital status: Married
Country: Vietnam

Gabriela Ramirez
Age: 26 years old
Marital status: Single
Country: Argentina

Write sentences about the pictures.

EXAMPLE: (Marital Status) Roberto ***is married***.

1. (Country) Duong and Nam ______________________________.
2. (Marital Status) Gabriela and Felipe ______________________________.
3. (Age) Nam ____________________ and Felipe ____________________.
4. (Country) Eva ____________________ and Roberto ____________________.

LESSON 3

Personal information

GOAL ▶ **Describe people** — *Vocabulary*

A **Look at Felipe's driver's license. Complete the sentences about Felipe.**

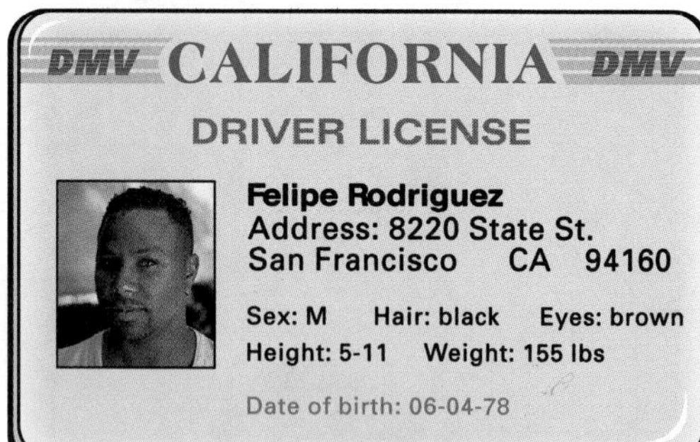

DMV CALIFORNIA DMV
DRIVER LICENSE
Felipe Rodriguez
Address: 8220 State St.
San Francisco CA 94160
Sex: M Hair: black Eyes: brown
Height: 5-11 Weight: 155 lbs
Date of birth: 06-04-78

We write: 5'11" **We say:** Five feet, eleven inches **or:** Five-eleven

1. Felipe is ____________ tall. (Height)
2. His weight is ______ pounds.
3. His hair is ____________ and his eyes are ____________.
4. He is ______ years old.
5. His address is ____________ State Street, San Francisco, CA ____________.

B **Make sentences about Duong and Eva.**

Duong	*Eva*
His hair is black.	**Her** hair is white.

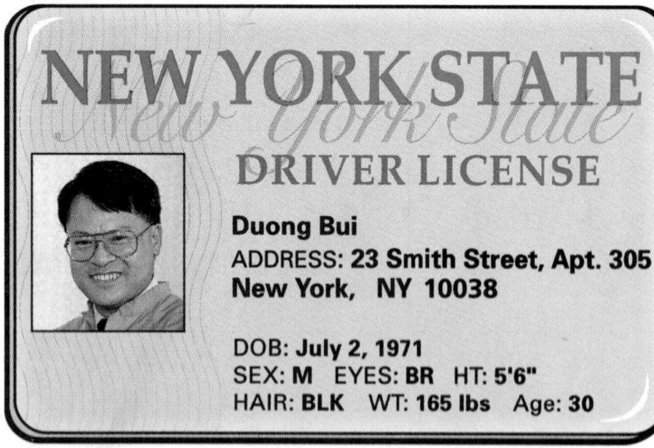

NEW YORK STATE
New York State
DRIVER LICENSE
Duong Bui
ADDRESS: 23 Smith Street, Apt. 305
New York, NY 10038
DOB: July 2, 1971
SEX: M EYES: BR HT: 5'6"
HAIR: BLK WT: 165 lbs Age: 30

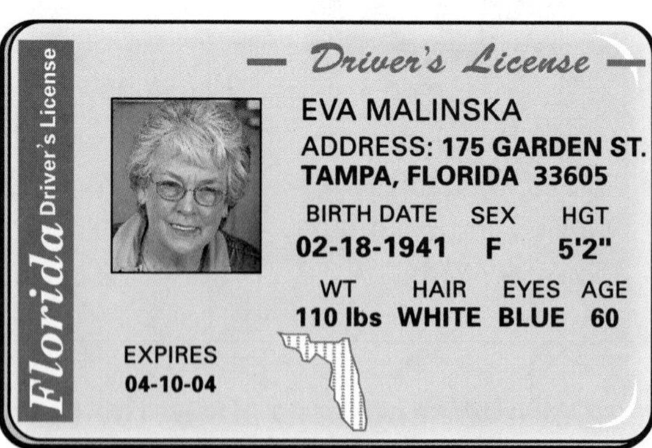

Florida Driver's License
— Driver's License —
EVA MALINSKA
ADDRESS: 175 GARDEN ST.
TAMPA, FLORIDA 33605
BIRTH DATE SEX HGT
02-18-1941 F 5'2"
WT HAIR EYES AGE
110 lbs WHITE BLUE 60
EXPIRES
04-10-04

1. Duong is ______________________
2. He ______________________
3. His ______________________
4. ______________________

1. Eva is ______________________
2. She ______________________
3. Her ______________________
4. ______________________

Ask your partner questions about the people on page 6. Then complete the chart below. Remember to use: *he, she, his, her.*

EXAMPLES:

How tall is Felipe?
What color are his eyes?
How old is he?
What is his weight?
What color is his hair?
What is his address?

Name	Height	Weight	Hair	Eyes	Age	Address
Felipe						
Duong						
Eva						

D **Complete the driver's license with your information.**

Driver's License

Name:______________ Age:__________

Weight:____________ Height:________

Hair:______________ Eyes:__________

Address:______________________________

City:______________ State:_________

Zip Code:______________

Your photo here

LESSON 4 What's your hairstyle?

GOAL ▶ Use the verb *have* **Grammar**

A Discuss these new words with your teacher.

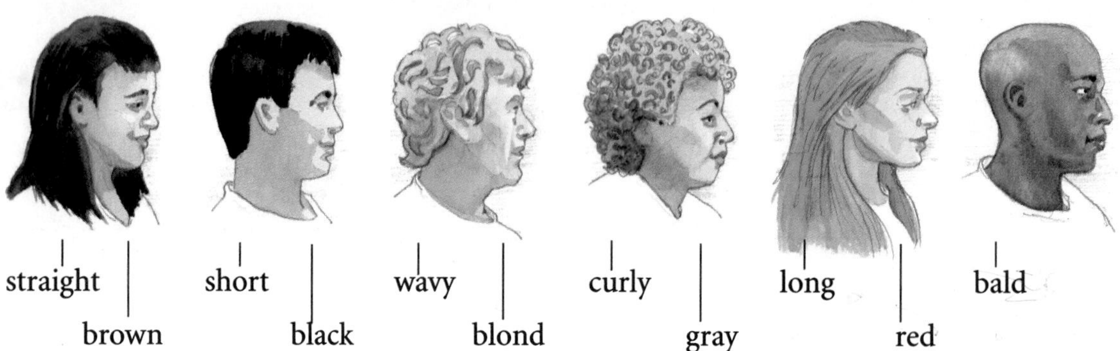

B In a group, choose and draw the best hair color and hairstyle for each face below.

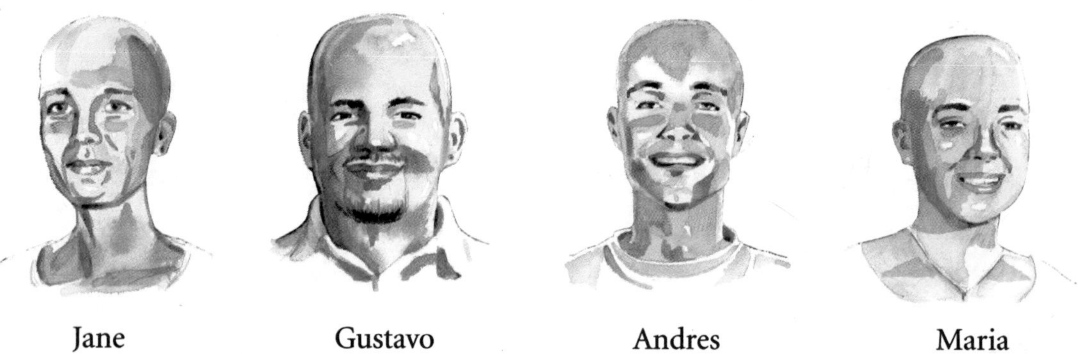

C Write your group's ideas below. Then share your ideas with the class.

EXAMPLE: Jane ***has*** wavy brown hair. Andres ***is*** bald.

1. ______________________________
2. ______________________________
3. ______________________________
4. ______________________________

D **Study the chart with your teacher.**

have		
Subject	**Verb**	**Example sentence**
I, you, we, they	have	I have short black hair. They have brown eyes.
he, she, it	has	She has long brown hair.

E **Write sentences about the students in Roberto's class. Look at the pictures on page 5 to find the information.**

EXAMPLE:
Roberto has short black hair and brown eyes.

1. Duong ______________________________.
2. Eva ______________________________.
3. Gabriela ______________________________.
4. Duong and Nam ______________________________.
5. Gabriela and Felipe ______________________________.

F **Describe a student in your class. Your partner can guess who it is.**

EXAMPLE:
Student A: She has short white hair.
Student B: It's Eva!

G **Write sentences about students in your class.**

EXAMPLE:
Sarina has long brown hair and green eyes.

1. ______________________________
2. ______________________________
3. ______________________________
4. ______________________________

Roberto's family

GOAL ▶ Describe families | ***Vocabulary***

Who is in the picture?
What are they saying?

Listen to the conversation.

Roberto: Mom and Dad, this is Duong. He is in my English class.
Antonio: Nice to meet you, Duong. Where are you from?
Duong: I'm from Vietnam.
Rebecca: I'm happy to meet you.
Duong: It's nice to meet you, too.
Roberto: Is Julio home?
Antonio: Your brother is at work, but your sister is with Silvia in the other room.

B **Make groups of three students and practice the conversation.**

Look at the picture and write the names on the family tree below. Then listen to Roberto and check your answers.

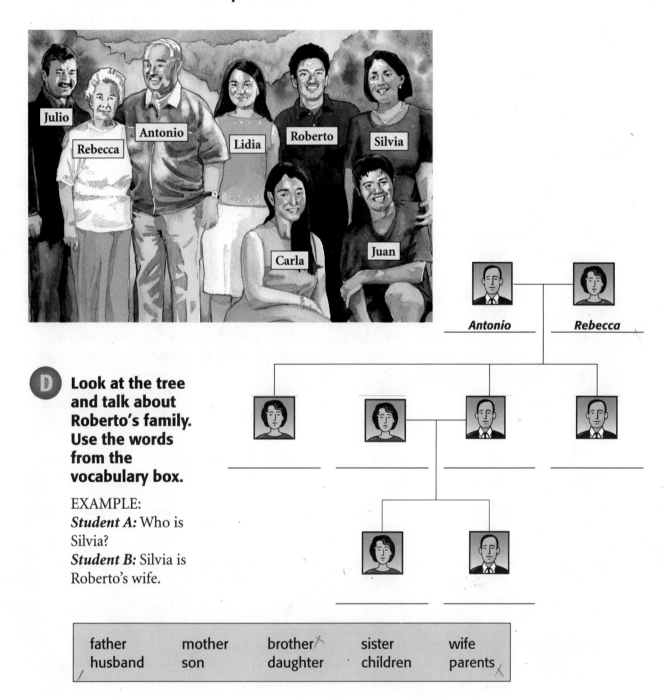

Julio
Rebecca
Antonio
Lidia
Roberto
Silvia
Carla
Juan

Antonio ______ *Rebecca* ______

______ ______ ______ ______

______ ______

D **Look at the tree and talk about Roberto's family. Use the words from the vocabulary box.**

EXAMPLE:
Student A: Who is Silvia?
Student B: Silvia is Roberto's wife.

father	mother	brother	sister	wife
husband	son	daughter	children	parents

E **On a separate piece of paper, draw a family tree with the first names of your parents, brothers, and sisters. Show it to a partner. Ask questions about your partner's chart.**

EXAMPLE:
Student A: Who is Elena? ***Student B:*** Elena is my sister.

F **Read Roberto's story and answer the questions.**

My name is Roberto. I am 43 years old. I'm married. My wife's name is Silvia. I have two children, Juan and Carla. Juan is 17 years old. He has straight black hair and brown eyes. Carla is 15. Carla has long, black hair and brown eyes. I love my family.

1. Is Roberto married? ____________
2. Does Roberto have children? ____________

G **Read Julio's story and answer the questions.**

My name is Julio. I'm single. My parents are wonderful. My father, Antonio, and my mother, Rebecca, have three children, Roberto, Lidia, and me. I am 45 years old. My brother Roberto is 43. He is tall and has short, black hair. My sister, Lidia, is 40 years old. I love my family very much.

1. Is Julio married? ____________
2. Does Julio have brothers and sisters? ____________

H **Write a paragraph about your family. Use the paragraphs about Roberto and Julio to help you. Bring a photograph of your family to go with your writing and show it to the class.**

____

____

____

____

____

I **Active Task:** Find examples of family tree charts in the library or on the Internet and show them to your class.

LESSON 6 I like sports and music.

GOAL ▶ Use *like* in the present tense — **Grammar**

Listen and put an "R" by things Roberto likes and an "S" by things Silvia likes.

movies ____

music ____

sports ____

games ____

computers ____

TV ____

books ***R***

restaurants ***S***

parks ____

B Complete these sentences.

1. Roberto likes ***books***.
2. Roberto likes ________________.
3. Roberto likes ________________.
4. Silvia likes ________________.
5. Silvia likes ________________.
6. Silvia likes ________________.
7. They both like ________________.
8. They both like ________________.

Study the chart with your teacher.

like			
Subject	**Verb**	**Noun**	**Example sentence**
I, you	like	movies	I like computers.
he, she, it	likes	music	She likes sports.
we, they	like	sports	They like music.
		games	
		computers	
		TV	
		books	
		restaurants	
		parks	

D Talk to a partner and write.

1. What do you like? I like ______________________. ______________________ ______________________	2. What does your partner like? He or she likes ______________________. ______________________ ______________________
3. What do you and your partner like? We both like ______________________. ______________________ ______________________	

E Introduce your partner to another pair.

EXAMPLE:

This is my friend Roberto. He is from Mexico. He is married and has two children. Roberto likes movies and books.

LESSON 7

When do you study?

GOAL ▶ Tell time

Life Skill

When does Roberto practice English? Look at the clocks and read the times.

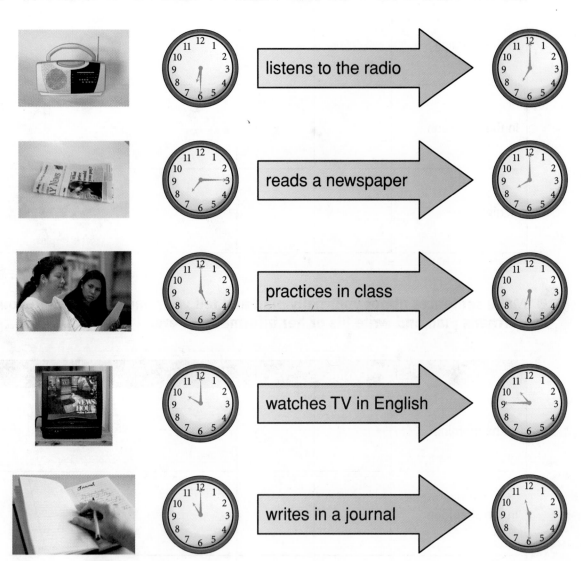

listens to the radio

reads a newspaper

practices in class

watches TV in English

writes in a journal

Make sentences about Roberto.

EXAMPLE: ***Roberto listens to the radio from six thirty to seven o'clock in the morning.***

1. He reads a newspaper from ***seven fifteen/7:15*** to ________________.

2. He ________________.

3. ________________.

4. ________________.

C When and how do you practice English every day? Fill in the chart with different ways to practice English.

	From	To	Activity
In the morning			
In the afternoon			
At night			

D Make sentences about your daily plan and tell your partner. Listen to your partner's plan and write his or her information here.

	From	To	Activity
In the morning			
In the afternoon			
At night			

E Make sentences about your partner's plan and tell the class.

Review

A **Fill in the circle next to the correct answer.**

EXAMPLE:
My name ______ Duong.
○ am ● is ○ are

1. I ______ from Vietnam.
   ○ am ○ is ○ are
2. Roberto ______ from Mexico.
   ○ am ○ is ○ are
3. Roberto and Duong ______ students.
   ○ am ○ is ○ are
4. Roberto and Duong both ______ black hair.
   ○ has ○ have ○ are
5. Roberto ______ one brother.
   ○ has ○ have ○ are
6. Silvia ______ computers.
   ○ likes ○ like ○ is like

B **What is their relationship? Look back at page 11 and fill in the missing words.**

EXAMPLE:
Roberto is Silvia's husband, and Silvia is Roberto's ***wife***.

1. Silvia is Juan's mother, and Juan is Silvia's ______________________.
2. Juan is Carla's brother, and Carla is Juan's ______________________.
3. Roberto is Carla's father, and Carla is Roberto's ______________________.
4. Roberto and Silvia are Juan and Carla's ______________________.
5. Juan and Carla are Roberto and Silvia's ______________________.

C **Match the questions and the answers. Write the correct letter next to each number.**

1. ***d*** What's your name?	a. 6 feet 2 inches.
2. ____ Where are you from?	b. 28.
3. ____ How old are you?	c. Yes, I am.
4. ____ What is your weight?	d. Ernesto Gonzalez.
5. ____ What is your height?	e. 145 pounds.
6. ____ Are you married?	f. Colombia.

Review

D **How does Roberto practice English? Fill in the missing words.**

1. He ________________ to the radio.
2. He ________________ TV.
3. He ________________ the newspaper.
4. He ________________ in his journal.

E **Write two other ways to practice English.**

1. ____
2. ____

F **What time is it? Write the time under each clock.**

1. It's ____________. 2. It's ____________. 3. It's ____________. 4. It's ____________.

G **Ask two students about their name, age, and marital status. Write sentences about the two students.**

EXAMPLE: Rieko is from Japan. She is 29 years old, and she is married.

1. ____
2. ____

H **Describe two people in your class. What color is his or her hair? What color are his or her eyes? Write one sentence about each person.**

1. ____
2. ____

TEAM PROJECT

Creating a student profile

In this project you will work together to create a student profile for each person in your team.

1. Form a team with four or five students.

   In your team, you need:

Position	Job	Student Name
Student 1 Leader	See that everyone speaks English. See that everyone participates.	
Student 2 Secretary	Complete the student profile with help from the team.	
Student 3	Give personal information for introductions.	
Students 4 and 5	Introduce student to other groups.	

2. Choose one student in your group to do a profile on.
3. Complete a student profile sheet by asking questions. Each student in the group asks three or more questions. (See page 17 for help.)
4. Write the information on the profile sheet. (See pages 6–9 for help.)
5. Practice introducing the student to the other groups. Use the profile sheet.
6. Repeat with other student profiles if you have time.

PRONUNCIATION

Practice the /h/ sound at the beginning of words. Listen and repeat.

he	his	here	husband	home
hair	how	who	height	her

LEARNER LOG

Circle what you learned and write the page number where you learned it.

1. I can talk about places and names.
   Yes Maybe No Page ______
2. I can find countries on a map.
   Yes Maybe No Page ______
3. I can introduce people.
   Yes Maybe No Page ______
4. I can describe people.
   Yes Maybe No Page ______
5. I can talk about families.
   Yes Maybe No Page ______
6. I can use the verb *be*.
   Yes Maybe No Page ______
7. I can talk about things I like.
   Yes Maybe No Page ______
8. I can tell the time.
   Yes Maybe No Page ______

Did you answer *No* to any questions? Review the information with a partner.

Rank what you like to do best from 1 to 6. 1 is your favorite activity. Your teacher will help you.

☐ practice listening

☐ practice speaking

☐ practice reading

☐ practice writing

☐ learn new words (vocabulary)

☐ learn grammar

In the next unit I want to practice more

______________________________.

UNIT 2

Let's Go Shopping

GOALS

- Talk about where to buy goods
- Count money and read receipts
- Identify clothing
- Use possessive adjectives
- Use adjectives to describe things
- Write checks
- Use *this, that, these,* and *those*

Shopping

GOAL ▶ Talk about where to buy goods ***Vocabulary***

A Read about Van.

Van starts school on Monday. She wants a dictionary,  sneakers,  new shirts,  a CD player,  and food for lunches. 

B Write Van's shopping items under the correct stores below.

24–7 Convenience Store

Martin's Department Store	24–7 Convenience Store	Sam's Food Mart	Hero's Books	Victory Shoes	Shop and Dress for Less
dictionary	______	______	*dictionary*	______	______
______	______	______	______	______	______

C What other things can you buy at each store? Make a list with a group.

Listen to Van and her husband. Draw a circle around where she goes.

Goods	Types of stores	
1. CD player	department store	convenience store
2. shoes	shoe store	department store
3. shirts	clothing store	department store
4. dictionary	bookstore	department store
5. bread, cheese, and fruit	supermarket	convenience store

E **In a group ask, "Where do you shop for clothes?" Make a list.**

________________ ________________ ________________

________________ ________________ ________________

F **Make a bar graph. How many students shop in different types of stores?**

EXAMPLE:

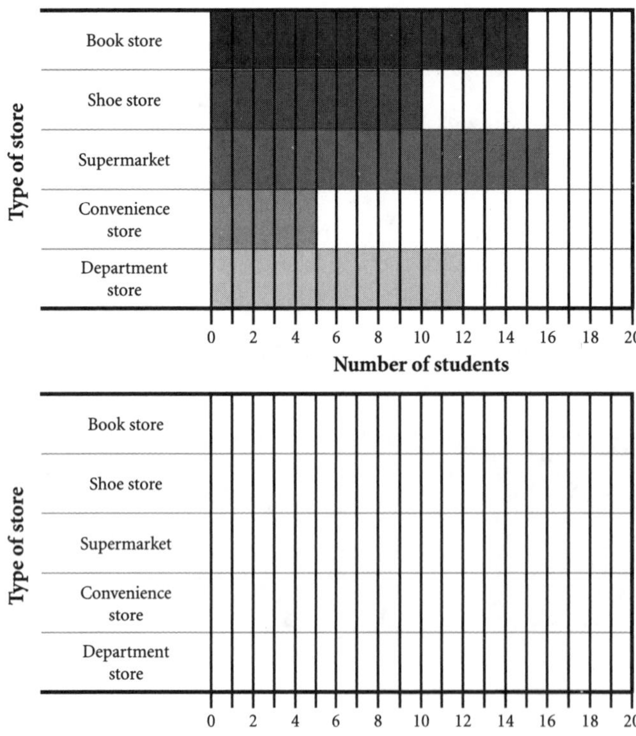

Active Task: Go to a mall or on the Internet. Find the names of three clothing stores. Report to the class.

LESSON 2 Van's purchases

GOAL ▶ **Count money and read receipts** — ***Life Skill***

Look at the receipts. What are the totals? What is the tax?

Martin's

SHIRTS 2 @ $17.98 –	$35.96
SNEAKERS –	$22.99
TAX –	$4.72
TOTAL –	$63.67

Hero's Books

BILINGUAL DICTIONARY–	$21.95
TAX –	$ 1.76
TOTAL –	$23.71

Sam's Food Mart

BREAD –	$ 2.30
CHEESE –	$ 2.75
ORANGES @ 60¢ A POUND –	$ 1.20
POTATO CHIPS –	$ 2.60
TOTAL –	$8.85

B How much is the total for the shirts, sneakers, bilingual dictionary, and food together with tax? Total ____________

C Listen and circle what you hear.

EXAMPLE:	$12.50	$ 2.15	($22.50)	$22.15
1. $35.15	$34.15	$34.50	$45.50	
2. $13.00	$30.00	$33.00	$43.00	
3. $.57	$57.00	$15.70	$17.00	
4. $19.75	$17.90	$79.00	$77.95	

D Listen and write the prices.

vacuum

$98.99

washing machine

$ ____________

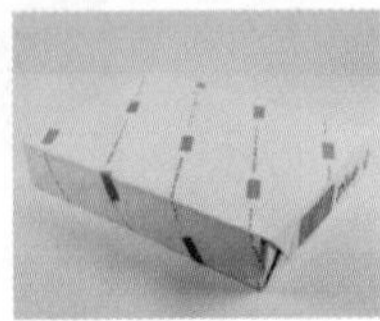
paper

$ ____________

candy bar

$ ____________

telephone

$ ____________

Practice asking about prices. Look at exercise D on page 23 for information.

EXAMPLE:
Student A: Excuse me, how much is the **vacuum**?
Student B: It's $98.99.
Student A: Thank you.

Look at the money. Write the words with the pictures.

a one-dollar bill	a five-dollar bill	a ten-dollar bill	a twenty-dollar bill
a quarter	a dime	a nickel	a penny

a one-dollar bill ____ ____ ____

____ ____ ____ ____

What bills and coins do you need for these items? Tell a partner and the class.

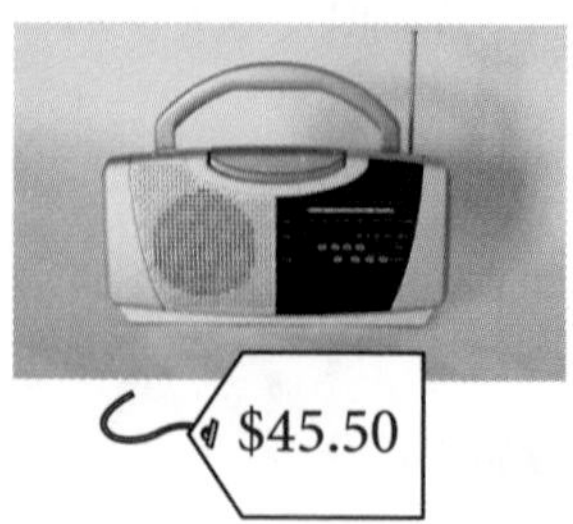

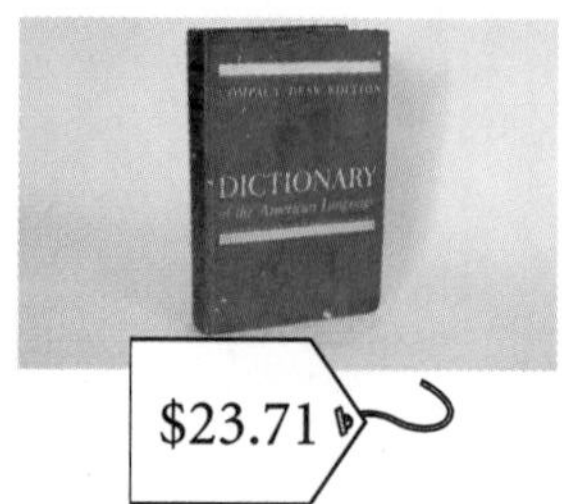

Active Task: Bring receipts from home and show the class.

LESSON 3 Buying new clothes

GOAL ▶ **Identify clothing** — **Vocabulary**

A **Write the correct letter under each type of clothing.**

a. suit	g. socks
b. T-shirt	h. baseball cap
c. ties	i. tennis shoes
d. hat	j. blouse
e. sweater	k. coat
f. dress	l. skirt

B **Write the clothing in the chart. Work in a group. Add other clothing words that you know.**

Women's	Men's	Both	

Where is Gabriela?
What is her problem?

C **Read about Gabriela's problem.**

Gabriela is worried. She needs new clothes for her job. She has $75 in cash, and she has a credit card. Is it a good idea to use a credit card?

D **Look at the ad on page 25. What can Gabriela buy with $75? What is the total before tax? Write the items and their prices. Then talk in a group.**

_______________ _______________ _______________

_______________ _______________ _______________

E **Active Task:** At home, find an ad in the newspaper or on the Internet. What clothing can you buy for $100?

LESSON 4 What color is your shirt?

GOAL ▶ Use possessive adjectives | *Grammar*

A **Say the clothes and colors with your teacher.**

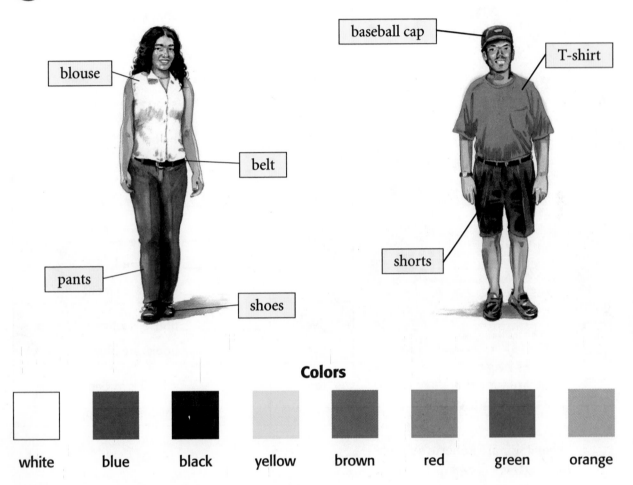

Colors

white, blue, black, yellow, brown, red, green, orange

B **Complete the chart with the words from the picture. Can you add any other clothing words?**

Singular	Plural	Plural only
T-shirt	*T-shirts*	*pants*

Study the chart with your teacher. Use the words in the box to complete the chart.

his	her
my	our
your	their
its	

Pronoun	Possessive adjectives
I	___*My*___ shirt is blue. __________ shoes are black.
you	__________ baseball cap is blue. __________ shorts are brown.
he	__________ belt is black. __________ sandals are brown.
she	__________ blouse is pink. __________ shoes are white.
it	__________ label is red. __________ doors are green.
we	__________ house is white. __________ books are blue.
they	__________ school is in Center City. __________ children are happy.

Look at page 27. Then answer the questions below.

EXAMPLE:
What color are Roberto's shorts?
His shorts are brown.

1. What color is Gabriela's blouse?

____

2. What color are Gabriela's and Roberto's belts?

____

3. What color are Gabriela's pants?

____

4. What color is Roberto's T-shirt?

____

5. What color are Gabriela's and Roberto's shoes?

____

Talk to a partner and describe the clothes of students in the class. Then write the sentences.

My (shirt) is ______________. ______________ ______________ ______________	Her (blouse) is ______________. ______________ ______________ ______________
His (shirt) is ______________. ______________ ______________ ______________	Their (shirts) are ______________. ______________ ______________ ______________
Your (shirt) is ______________. ______________ ______________ ______________	Our (shirts) are ______________. ______________ ______________ ______________

F **With a different partner, describe students in the class by their clothes and guess who they are.**

EXAMPLE:
Student A: Her blouse is blue.
Student B: It's Amy!

G **Look around the classroom. In groups, make a list of clothes by color.**

Red	Blue	Green	Orange

LESSON 5 A big TV or a small TV?

GOAL ▶ Use adjectives to describe things — *Vocabulary*

Look at the pictures. Write the correct adjective under each picture.

Do you want a small CD player or a large CD player?

small ______ *large* ______

Do you want an old house or a new house?

______ ______

Do you want a new car or a used car?

______ ______

Do you want a striped shirt or a checked shirt?

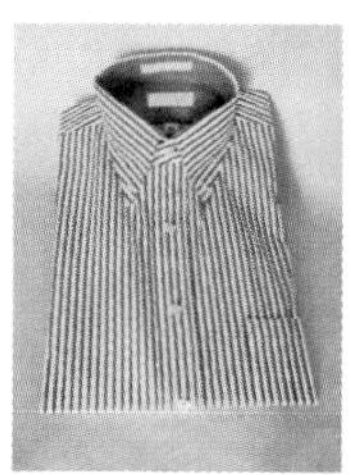

______ ______

Do you want a large blouse or a medium blouse?

______ ______

Do you want a small shirt or a medium shirt?

______ ______

B Complete the chart. Write the new words.

Size	Age	Pattern
small	*used*	*striped*

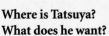

Where is Tatsuya?
What does he want?

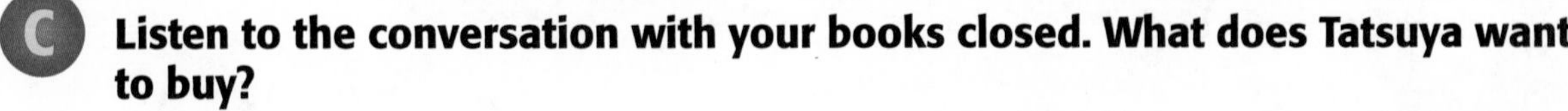

C Listen to the conversation with your books closed. What does Tatsuya want to buy?

Tatsuya: Excuse me, I want a TV.
Salesperson: A big TV or a small TV?
Tatsuya: I want a large TV for my bedroom.
Salesperson: Okay, how about this one?
Tatsuya: Yes, that's good. How much is it?
Salesperson: It's $135.00.
Tatsuya: I'll take it!

D Practice the conversation with a partner.

E Practice new conversations using the information below.

Student A is the customer. Student B is the salesperson.	Student B is the customer. Student A is the salesperson.
1. Blouse: medium / small	1. Car: used / new
2. CD player: large / small	2. House: old / new
3. Refrigerator: new / used	3. Sweater: striped / checked
4. Shirt: small / medium	4. Blouse: large / medium

F Write a new conversation with a partner.

LESSON 6 Cash, check, or charge?

GOAL ▶ Write checks

Life Skill

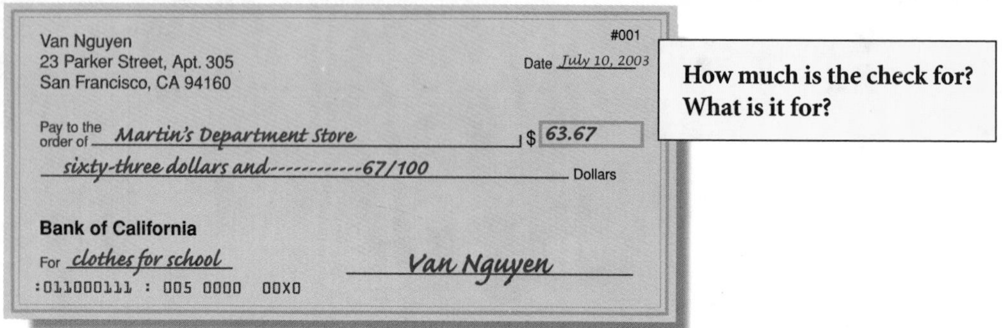

How much is the check for?
What is it for?

A Read about banks with your teacher.

It is a good idea to put your money in the bank. It is not a good idea to carry a lot of cash with you. When you want to use your money, you can take the money out of the bank, or you can write a check. Many people buy things in the United States with cash, checks, or credit cards.

B Circle *True* or *False*.

1. People use checks to buy things in the United States. True False
2. It is not a good idea to put money in the bank. True False
3. It is a good idea to carry a lot of cash with you. True False

C Write a check for a new TV to Al's Big Screen for $350.00.

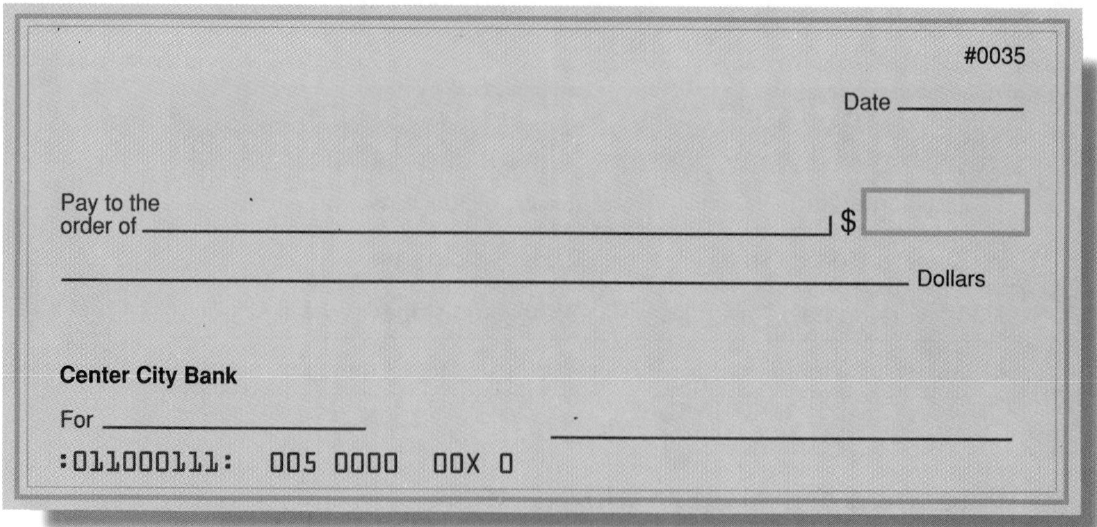

D **Read the checks.**

Check 1

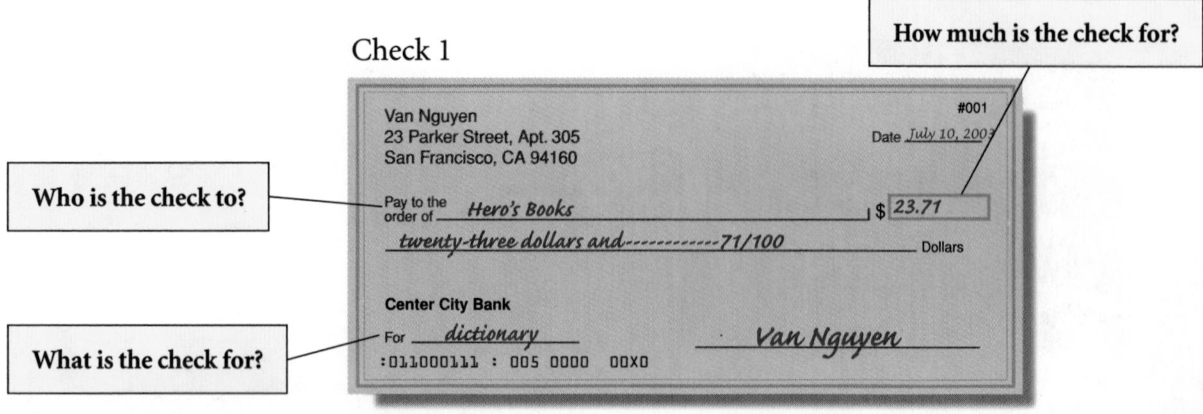

How much is the check for?
Van Nguyen
23 Parker Street, Apt. 305
San Francisco, CA 94160
#001
Date July 10, 2003
Who is the check to?
Pay to the order of Hero's Books
$ 23.71
twenty-three dollars and-----------71/100 Dollars
Center City Bank
What is the check for?
For dictionary
Van Nguyen
:011000111 : 005 0000 00X0

Check 2

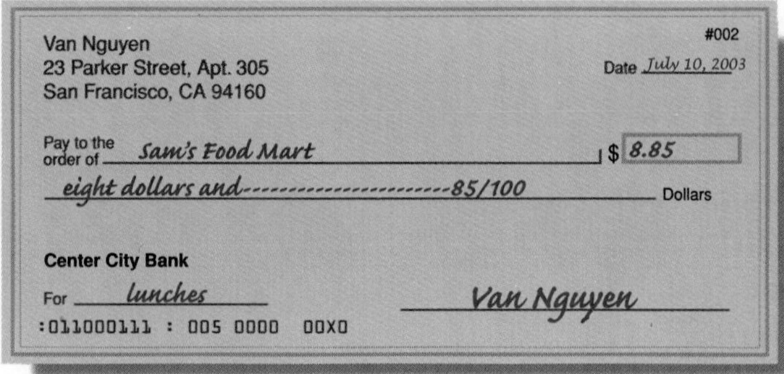

Van Nguyen
23 Parker Street, Apt. 305
San Francisco, CA 94160
#002
Date July 10, 2003
Pay to the order of Sam's Food Mart
$ 8.85
eight dollars and---------------------85/100 Dollars
Center City Bank
For lunches
Van Nguyen
:011000111 : 005 0000 00X0

E **Ask your partner. Listen and write the answers.**

1. Student A covers checks and asks questions.
2. Student B covers checks and asks questions.

Check #	Who is the check to?	What is the check for?	How much is the check for?
Check #1	Hero's Books		
Check #2			

F **Active Task:** Visit a bank or look on the Internet and find the names of three banks where you can open a checking account.

LESSON 7 Which umbrella do you want?

GOAL ▶ Use *this, that, these,* and *those* **Grammar**

Where is Roberto?
Who is talking to Roberto?

 **A Listen to the first part of the conversation. What does Roberto want to buy?**

______________________ ______________________

  **Listen to the next part of the conversation. What does Roberto want to buy?**

______________________ ______________________

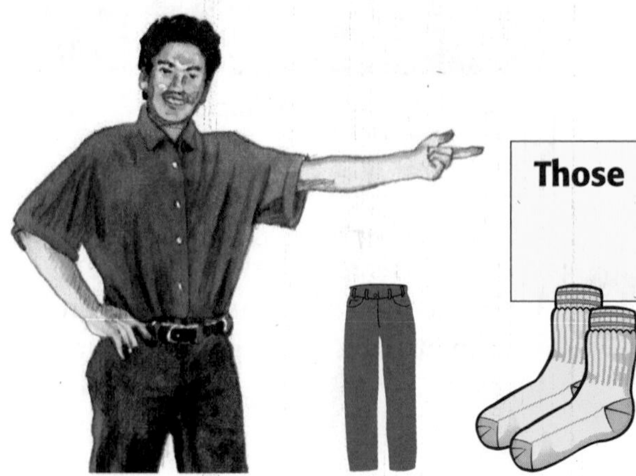

C Study the chart with your teacher.

	Near the speaker	Far from the speaker
Singular	this	that
Plural	these	those

D Look at the pictures on page 34 and fill in the missing words below.

EXAMPLE:
Roberto: "***This*** cap is orange and ***that*** cap is yellow."

1. __________ cap is yellow and __________ cap is orange.
2. __________ umbrella is __________ and __________ umbrella is green.
3. __________ jeans are blue and __________ jeans are __________.
4. __________ socks are __________ and __________ socks are yellow .

E Ask your partner five questions about the clothes in your classroom. Use *this, that, these, those.*

EXAMPLE:

Student A: What color is that shirt?
Student B: It's blue.

Student B: What color are these pants?
Student A: They're black.

F **Read the conversation.**

Salespeson: Can I help you?
Roberto: How much is this radio, please?
Salesperson: It's $8.65.
Roberto: How about that radio?
Salesperson: It's $48.
Roberto: I'll take this radio, please.

G **Practice new conversations with the pictures below.**

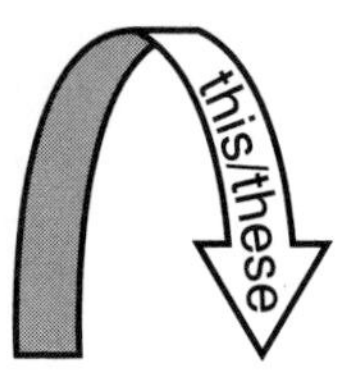

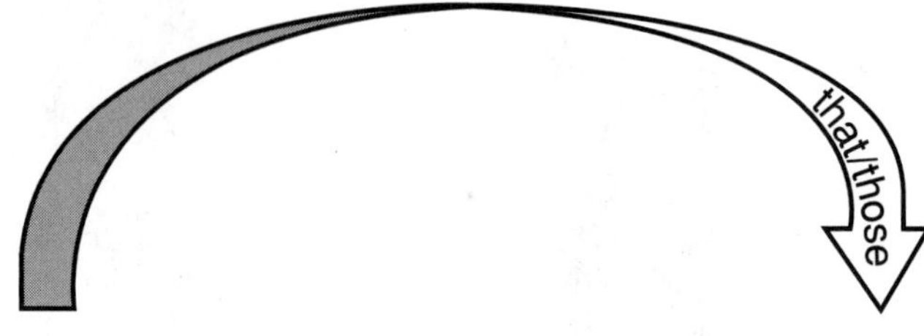

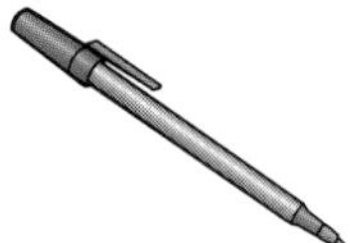

pen $0.89

pen $8.00

TV $225.50

TV $115.00

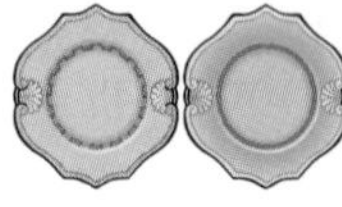

dishes $58.98

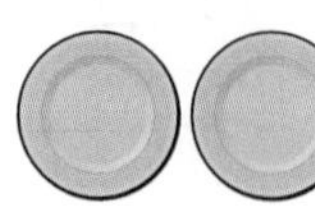

dishes $28.99

movie tickets $17.98

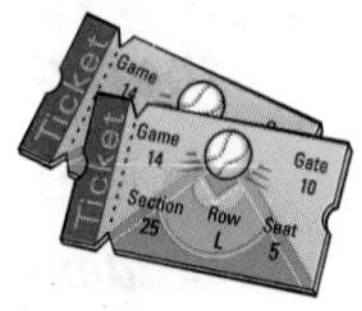

baseball tickets $22.00

Review

A **Listen and write the answers in column 1.**

B **Complete columns 2 and 3 with your ideas.**

Item	1. How much is it?	2. Where can you buy it?	3. Describe it.
		department store	*black and white*
	$168.00		
DICTIONARY	$18.75		
Size 12	$98.98		
	$456.78		
MMM	$23.99		
SSS	$17.00		
LLL	$24.50		

C Look at the receipt. What is the total? Fill in the correct amounts on the check.

Martin's Department Store

Men's shirts 2@ $27.98	$	______
Men's pants	$	65.49
Tax	$	4.48
Total	$	______

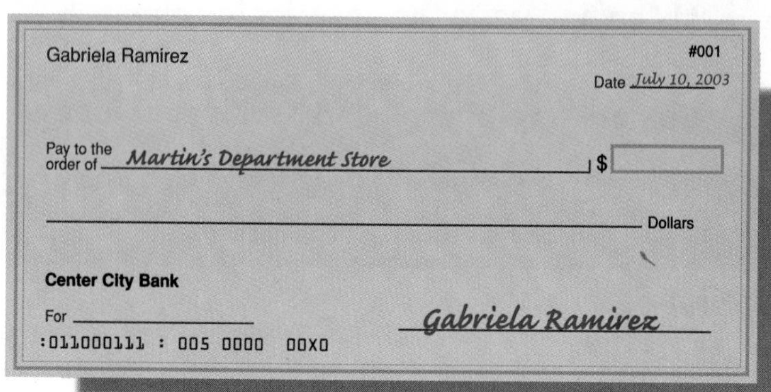
Gabriela Ramirez #001
Date *July 10, 2003*

Pay to the order of *Martin's Department Store* $ ______

______ Dollars

Center City Bank

For ______ *Gabriela Ramirez*

:011000111 : 005 0000 00X0

D Describe the pictures. Use *his, her,* or *their*.

EXAMPLE:
What color is Eva's hat? ***Her hat is blue.***

1. What color is Duong's cap? ______________________.
2. What color is Duong's shirt? ______________________.
3. What color are Eva's pants? ______________________.
4. What color are Eva's and Duong's shoes? ______________________.

TEAM PROJECT

Planning a department store

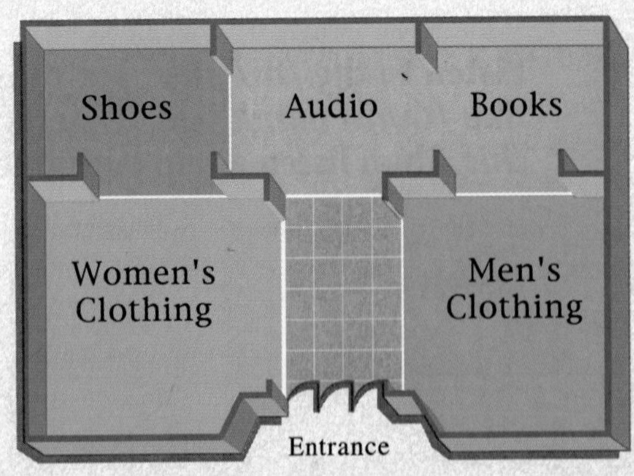

In this project you will plan a department store, decide what to sell, and present it to the class.

1. Form a team with four or five students.

   In your team, you need:

Position	Job	Student Name
Student 1 Leader	See that everyone speaks English. See that everyone participates.	
Student 2 Architect	With help from the team, draw the floor plan.	
Student 3 Sales manager	List the sales prices.	
Student 4 Writer	With help from the team, prepare a skit to present to the class.	

2. Choose a name for your department store.
3. Choose one floor of your department store. Draw the floor plan.
4. Make a list of ten things you sell, with their prices. Where are they located on your floor plan?
5. Prepare a skit in which a person in your group talks to a salesperson and buys some things. You can also make checks and receipts if you want. People in your group can be: a salesperson, a cashier, a customer or customers, and a manager.
6. Practice the skit and present it to the class.

PRONUNCIATION

Listen to the /th/ sound in these words. Circle the words which sound like /th/ in *thank you*. Underline the words which sound like /th/ in *this*. Then listen again and repeat.

think	these	thirty	those	theater	brother	thing
mother	clothing	with	bath	three	father	path

LEARNER LOG

Circle what you learned and write the page number where you learned it.

1. I know where to shop.
   Yes Maybe No Page ______
2. I can identify clothing.
   Yes Maybe No Page ______
3. I can read receipts.
   Yes Maybe No Page ______
4. I can count money.
   Yes Maybe No Page ______
5. I can write a check.
   Yes Maybe No Page ______
6. I can describe things.
   Yes Maybe No Page ______
7. I can use possessive adjectives.
   Yes Maybe No Page ______
8. I can use *this, that, these,* and *those.*
   Yes Maybe No Page ______

Did you answer *No* to any questions? Review the information with a partner.

Rank what you like to do best from 1 to 6. 1 = your favorite activity. Your teacher will help you.

- ☐ practice listening
- ☐ practice speaking
- ☐ practice reading
- ☐ practice writing
- ☐ learn new words (vocabulary)
- ☐ learn grammar

In the next unit I want to practice more

____

______________________________.

UNIT 3

Food

GOALS

- Talk about eating habits and meals
- Read and follow instructions
- Read a menu and order food
- Use count and non-count nouns
- Use the simple present
- Compare prices
- Read a recipe

LESSON 1 What's for lunch?

GOAL ▶ Talk about eating habits and meals — *Vocabulary*

A Read about Dave.

I'm Dave Chen. I'm an English teacher in Florida. I like to eat! I eat a big breakfast in the morning, a small lunch at noon, and a big dinner around six o'clock.

Where is Dave? What kind of food does he eat?

B Write the names of the food from the picture in the chart below.

Breakfast	Lunch	Dinner
AM	PM *pizza*	PM

C **What time do you eat breakfast? Make a bar graph with your class.**

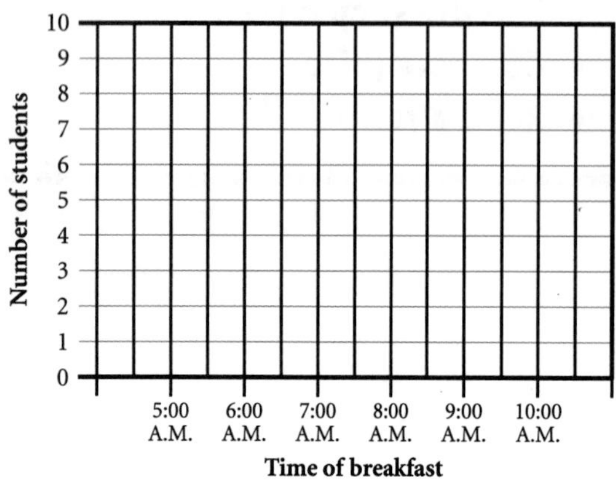

beans and rice

tacos

fried noodles

egg rolls

roast beef

spaghetti

D **What do you eat for breakfast, lunch, and dinner? Ask your teacher for words you don't know.**

Breakfast	Lunch	Dinner

E **Ask your partner what he or she eats for breakfast, lunch, and dinner.**

EXAMPLE:
Student A: What do you eat for dinner? ***Student B:*** I eat spaghetti and salad for dinner.

F **Tell the class about your partner.**

LESSON 2 Using a vending machine

GOAL ▶ Read and follow instructions *Life Skill*

Natasha gets her lunch every day after class from a vending machine at school.

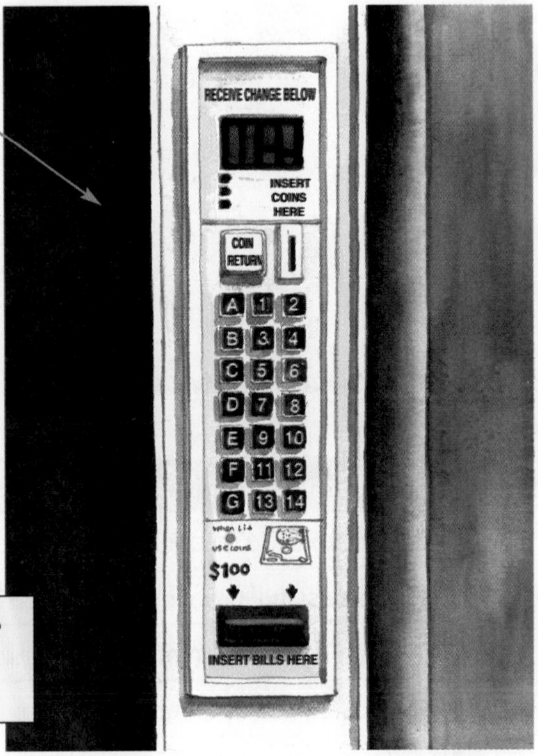

What is in the vending machine? Do you eat from a vending machine sometimes?

A Look at the vending machine. Listen and write a number by each sentence when you hear it.

_____ Put your dollar bills in this slot.

_____ Take your change.

_____ Choose the number.

__*1*__ Decide what you want.

B Can you give a partner the directions without looking at the sentences?

C **Work in pairs. Ask questions about the prices of items and explain how to use the vending machine.**

D **How much money do you need? Complete the chart.**

Selection	Total	Code
Ex. potato chips, peanuts, and gum	*$2.50*	*C1, B2, A3*
1. pretzels and a chocolate bar		
2. granola bar and mints		
3. cookies, trail mix, and gum		
4. peanuts, pretzels, and cookies		

E **Active Task:** Go to a vending machine in your school or neighborhood. Write down the instructions and bring them to class.

LESSON 3 Buying lunch

GOAL ▶ Read a menu and order food — **Vocabulary**

 **Study the menu on the lunch truck with your teacher.**

Sebastien buys his lunch every day from the lunch truck.

  **Listen to the orders. Write the order for each student below.**

1. Sebastien's order

Selection	Section	Price
cola	*beverages*	
cheeseburger	*sandwiches*	
	Total	

2. Tran's order

Selection	Section	Price
ham sandwich		
	Total	

3. Miyuki's order

Selection	Section	Price
	Total	

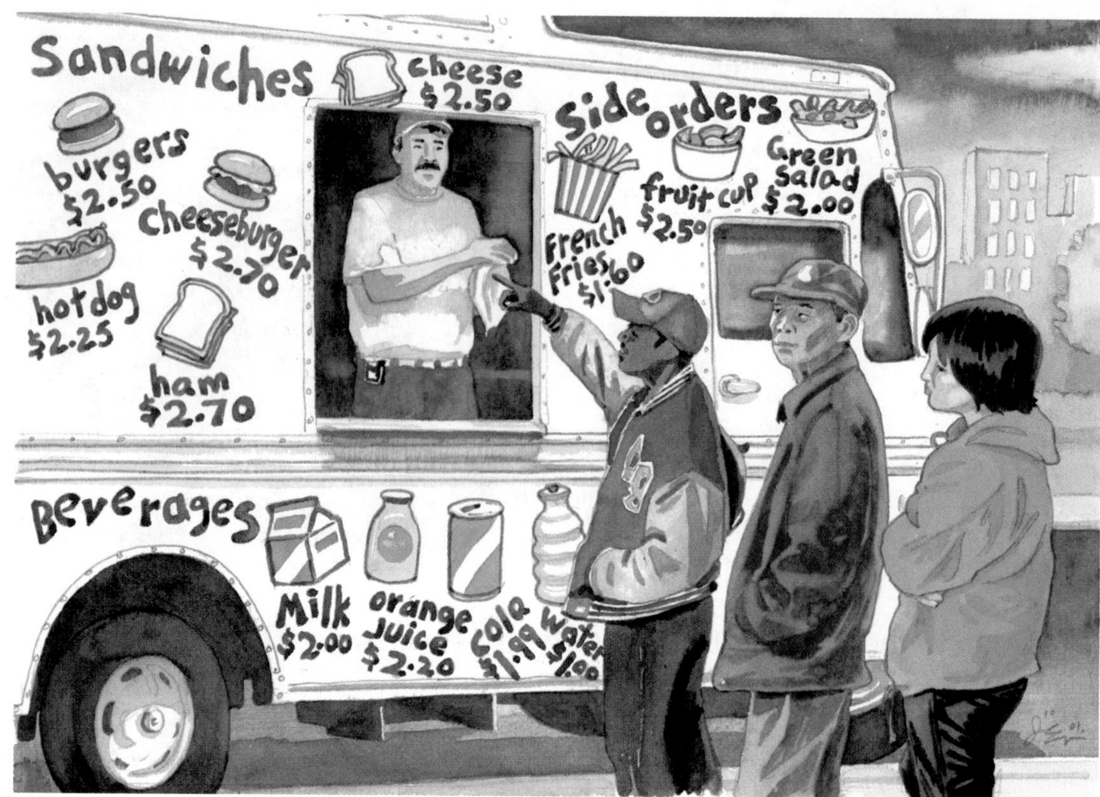

C **Practice the conversation with the class.**

Sebastien: Hi! I want a cheeseburger.
Server: A cheeseburger?
Sebastien: Yes, please. No onions. And a soda, please.
Server: OK, that's a cheeseburger and a soda.
Sebastien: That's right, thanks.

D **Practice the conversation again with new information.**

1. Ham sandwich with no tomato, French fries, and milk.

   Student A: Hi! I want a ______________________________.

2. Hot dog with no mustard, fruit cup, and water.

   Student B: Hi! I want a ______________________________.

E **Make your own conversations with a different partner. Use the menu on the lunch truck.**

F **Active Task:** Go to a lunch truck or cafeteria and order your lunch in English.

LESSON 4 How much are the oranges?

GOAL ▶ Use count and non-count nouns **Grammar**

Where is Duong?
What is he eating?

A **Read Duong's story.**

My name is Duong. I'm from Vietnam. I study at North Creek Adult School. It is very expensive to eat out every day so I bring my lunch to school. My wife and I go to the store every Saturday. We buy bread and meat for my sandwiches.

B **Answer the questions. Fill in the circle for *True* or *False*.**

	True	False
1. Duong buys his lunch at school.	○	○
2. Duong and his son go to the store every Saturday.	○	○
3. Duong and his wife buy bread and meat for sandwiches.	○	○

C **With a group, make a list of food for sandwiches that you can buy at the supermarket.**

________________ ________________ ________________

________________ ________________ ________________

________________ ________________ ________________

D **Study the advertisement with your teacher.**

MORE GROCERY SAVINGS FROM FOOD CITY
Bread
$1.98
Ground Beef
$2.25 a pound
Peanut Butter
$3.25
Cucumbers
$.68 each
Spaghetti
$1.25 per package
Tomatoes
$.68 a pound
Milk
$3.25 per gallon
Avocados
$1.25 each
Oranges
$.69 each
Cookies
$2.75
Mustard
$1.89
Potato chips
$2.75
Apples
$1.49 a pound
Cola
$2.69
Carrots
$1.00 a pound
Yogurt
$.79

E **Look at the advertisement. Which food items can you count? Your teacher will help.**

Count nouns	Non-count nouns

F **Ask your partner about the prices of the food.**

EXAMPLES:

Student A: How much is the peanut butter?
Student B: It's $3.25.

Student B: How much are the oranges?
Student A: They are 69 cents each.

G **Study the following words for food containers. Write the correct word under each picture.**

bag	bottle	can	jar	box	package

a ______ of soup

a ______ of water

a ______ of cheese

a ______ of cookies

a ______ of mustard

a ______ of potato chips

H **What other food goes into each kind of container?**

Container	Food
can	*coffee, beans*
bottle	
package	
box	
jar	
bag	

I **What food do you need today? Make a shopping list of six items.**

______ ______

______ ______

______ ______

LESSON 5 Who has the best lunch?

A **Read about Natasha, Sebastien, and Duong again. When and where do they eat lunch? Who has the best lunch?**

Natasha gets her lunch every day from a vending machine at school. Sebastien buys his lunch every day from the lunch truck. Duong brings his lunch every day in a paper bag and eats after class.

B **Study the chart with your teacher.**

Simple present		
Subject	**Verb**	**Example sentence**
I, you, we, they	bring	I **bring** my lunch.
	eat	You **eat** after class.
	get	We **get** our lunch from the store.
	buy	They **buy** lunch at the cafeteria.
he, she, it	bring**s**	He **brings** his lunch.
	get**s**	She **gets** her lunch from the store.
	eat**s**	It **eats** dog food.

C **Do you bring or buy lunch? Write a complete sentence.**

____

D **Talk to four students in the class. Ask: Do you bring or buy lunch? Write sentences.**

EXAMPLE:
I buy bread and fruit at the convenience store.

1. ____
2. ____
3. ____
4. ____

E **Read the advertisement with your teacher.**

PUENTE MARKET
COLA
$2.99
a bottle
Spaghetti
99¢
a package
MIRALAGO PASTA
Carrots
$1.25
a pound
Ground Beef
$1.99
a pound
Peanut Butter
$3.25
a jar
GOOBERS BEST
CREAMY
MILK
MILK
$3.20
a gallon
Tomatoes
$.60
a pound
Avocados
$.99
each

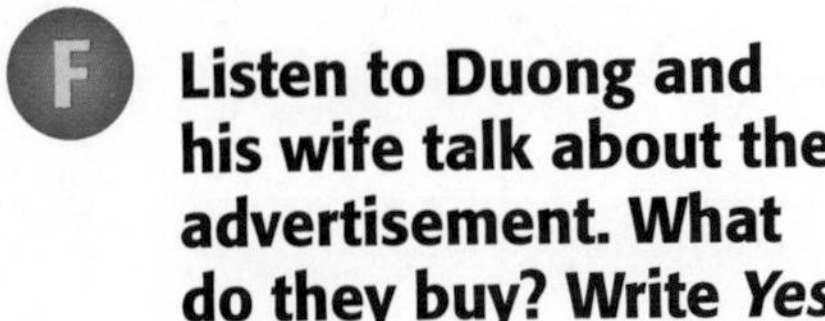

F **Listen to Duong and his wife talk about the advertisement. What do they buy? Write *Yes* or *No*.**

Yes/No	Item
Yes	ground beef
	spaghetti
	milk
	carrots
	tomatoes
	peanut butter
	cola
	avocados

G **Write sentences about what Duong and Minh buy.**

EXAMPLE: ***They buy ground beef.***

1. ______________________________

2. ______________________________

3. ______________________________

H Study the chart with your teacher.

Negative simple present			
Subject	**do + not**	**Base**	**Example sentence**
I you we they	do not (don't)	bring eat get buy	I don't bring sandwiches for lunch.
he she it	does not (doesn't)	bring eat get buy	He doesn't eat pizza for dinner.

I Write sentences about what Duong and Minh don't buy.

1. *They don't buy* ________________.
2. ________________.
3. ________________.

J Write three things that you and your partner don't like and don't buy.

I don't buy ________.	My partner doesn't like ________.
I don't like ________.	My partner doesn't buy ________.

LESSON 6 Which store is cheaper?

GOAL ▶ Compare prices — *Life Skill*

Look at Duong's shopping list. Look at the advertisement on page 48 for Food City and the advertisement on page 51 for Puente Market. Which store is cheaper for Duong? Talk in a group.

Shopping list

- ground beef
- tomatoes
- avocados
- carrots

B Study the graph. Fill in the missing information.

		($2.25)						
$2.25	($1.99)							
$2.00								
$1.75								
$1.50			($1.25)					
$1.25				($1.00)				
$1.00								
$.75								
$.50								
	ground beef		carrots		avocados		tomatoes	

KEY
- Puente
- Food City

Use the graph to practice comparing prices.

EXAMPLE:
Student A: I need some ground beef. Where is it cheaper?
Student B: It's cheaper at Puente Market.

Student B: I need some carrots. Where are they cheaper?
Student A: They're cheaper at Food City.

D **Look at the three bottles. How much is each bottle? Look at the unit price for each bottle. Which bottle is cheaper by the ounce?**

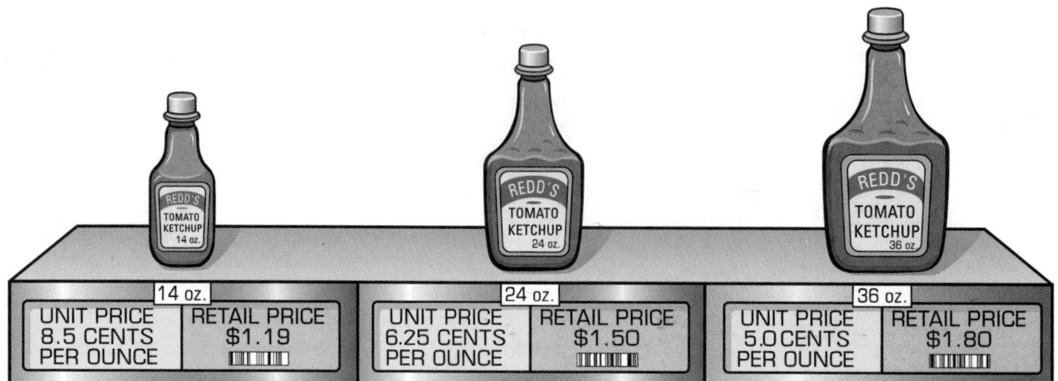

E **Look at the pictures above and practice.**

EXAMPLE:
Student A: How much is the fourteen-ounce bottle?
Student B: It's one dollar and nineteen cents.
That's eight point five cents an ounce.

oz = ounce
lb = pound
16 oz = 1 lb
8 pints = 1 gallon

F **Look at the chart and compare prices. Ask your partner: Which can of coffee is cheaper by the ounce?**

Coffee	Ice Cream	Cereal
8 oz $1.99 24.9 per ounce	1 pint $0.81 $6.48 per gallon	15 oz $2.19 14.6 per ounce
1 lb $2.99 18.7 per ounce	half gallon $1.99 $3.98 per gallon	20 oz $2.49 12.5 per ounce
24 oz $3.99 16.7 per ounce	1 gallon $3.49 $3.49 per gallon	25 oz $4.49 18 per ounce

G **Active Task:** As a class, choose one type of food. Choose two stores in your neighborhood or go to the Internet. Compare prices and tell the class which store is cheaper.

LESSON 7 Following instructions

GOAL ▶ Read a recipe

Vocabulary

A **Read the recipe for mashed potatoes with your class.**

Mashed potatoes: Serves 6.

Ingredients: 6 potatoes, 2 tablespoons of butter or margarine, 1 teaspoon of salt, garlic salt to taste, 1/4 cup of milk. **Instructions:** Peel and chop potatoes. Boil water. Add potatoes to boiling water. Cook for 10 minutes. Drain. Mix all ingredients. Whip with a whisk or a blender.

B **Read the recipe and write the correct number next to each picture. Then match the pictures with the words.**

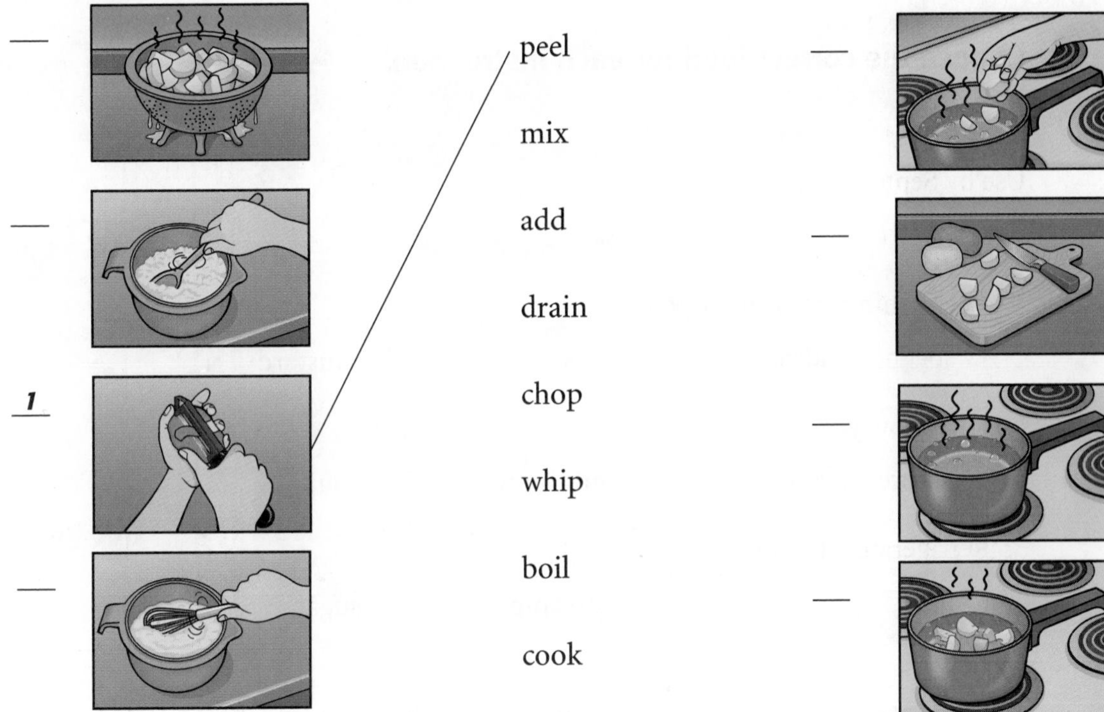

C **What other food words can go with these verbs?**

boil	***eggs, rice***	peel	________	chop	________
add	________	cook	________	whip	________

GOAL ▶ Read a recipe

Vocabulary

 **Study the charts with your teacher.**

Imperative verbs		
(You)	**Base**	**Example sentence**
	drain	Drain the water.
	chop	Chop the potatoes.
	peel	Peel the potatoes.

Negative imperative verbs			
(You)	**do + not**	**Base**	**Example sentence**
	do not	boil	Do not boil the water.
	(don't)	use	Do not use if seal is broken.
		cook	Do not cook in microwave.

E **Choose the correct food for each instruction.**

EXAMPLE:

Use by September 3.

○ spaghetti ● beef ○ salt

1. Use within 5 days after opening.

   ○ spaghetti sauce ○ carrots ○ mustard

2. Heat slowly.

   ○ ice cream ○ peanut butter ○ soup

3. Refrigerate after opening.

   ○ milk ○ potato chips ○ sugar

 **Active Task:** Find an easy recipe from a cookbook or from the Internet. Tell the class.

Review

A **Write the names of these foods. Are they for breakfast, lunch, or dinner?**

Breakfast	Lunch	Dinner

B **Talk to a partner about what he or she eats for breakfast, lunch, and dinner.**

C **You are in your school cafeteria. Order some of the food items from exercise A. Make a conversation with your partner.**

D **Give instructions on how to use a vending machine. Match the verbs with the instructions below.**

1. _____ what you want.
2. _____ the number.
3. _____ your dollar bills in the slot.
4. _____ your change.

a. Take
b. Put
c. Decide
d. Choose

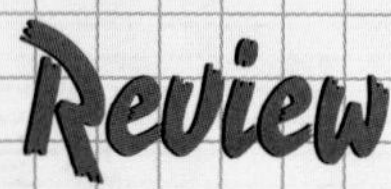

E Complete the chart.

Food	Count	Non-count	Container/Measurement
cereal		*x*	*box*
tomatoes			
cookies			
mustard			
potato chips			
soup			
water			

F Write four kinds of food you like and four kinds of food you don't like. Write complete sentences.

1. ***I like*** ____________________
2. ____________________
3. ____________________
4. ____________________
5. ***I don't like*** ____________________
6. ____________________
7. ____________________
8. ____________________

G Write four kinds of food your partner doesn't like. Write complete sentences.

1. ____________________
2. ____________________
3. ____________________
4. ____________________

TEAM PROJECT

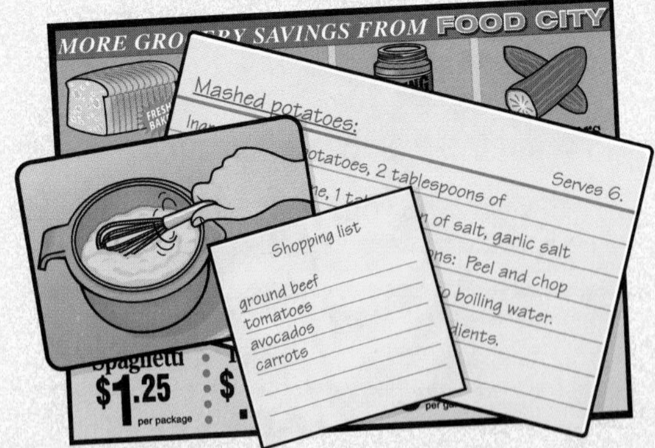

Writing a secret recipe

In this project you will write a recipe and make a shopping list.

1. Form a team with four or five students.

   In your team, you need:

Position	Job	Student Name
Student 1 Leader	See that everyone speaks English. See that everyone participates.	
Student 2 Chef	With help from the team, write a recipe.	
Student 3 Shopping manager	With help from the team, make a shopping list.	
Student 4 Budget manager	Advise your team on prices of food items.	

2. Choose a recipe and put it on an index card or on a piece of paper. Include the servings, ingredients, and instructions, but don't write its name! (See page 55 for help.)
3. Make a shopping list of the food you need. Include quantities and prices. (See page 49 for help.)
4. Give the recipe card and the shopping list to other groups. Ask them to guess what the recipe is for.

PRONUNCIATION

Can you hear the sounds /j/ and /y/ in these words? Listen and repeat.

jar	jelly	juice	package	orange	margarine
yes	yogurt	use	mayonnaise	menu	papaya

LEARNER LOG

Circle what you learned and write the page number where you learned it.

1. I can talk about meals and food.
   Yes Maybe No Page ______
2. I can use a vending machine.
   Yes Maybe No Page ______
3. I can read a menu.
   Yes Maybe No Page ______
4. I can place an order.
   Yes Maybe No Page ______
5. I can read an advertisement.
   Yes Maybe No Page ______
6. I can use count and non-count nouns.
   Yes Maybe No Page ______
7. I can comparison shop.
   Yes Maybe No Page ______
8. I can read a recipe.
   Yes Maybe No Page ______

Did you answer *No* to any questions? Review the information with a partner.

Rank what you like to do best from 1 to 6. 1 is your favorite activity. Your teacher will help you.

- ☐ practice listening
- ☐ practice speaking
- ☐ practice reading
- ☐ practice writing
- ☐ learn new words (vocabulary)
- ☐ learn grammar

In the next unit I want to practice more

______________________________.

UNIT 4

Housing

GOALS

- Identify types of housing
- Talk about rooms in a home
- Read and interpret classified ads
- Use the present continuous
- Use prepositions of location
- Understand a family budget
- Make a family budget

LESSON 1 What type of home do you have?

GOAL ▶ Identify types of housing — *Vocabulary*

A **Read the information about housing in Corbin. Then complete the chart and fill in the total.**

Housing Statistics: Corbin, CA

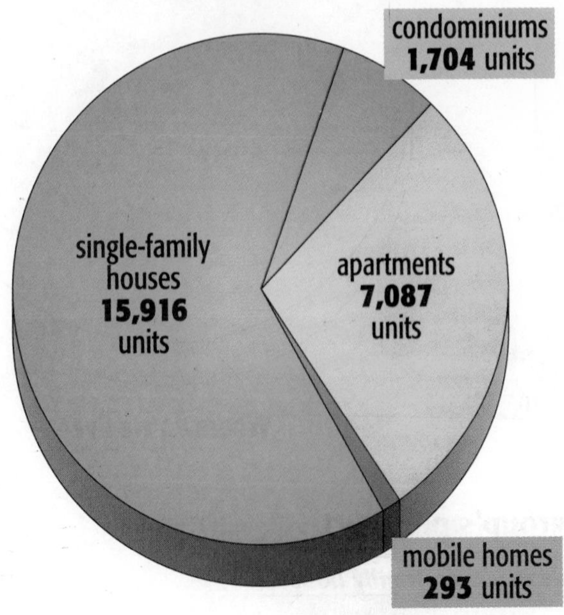

Type of housing	Number of units
	________
	________
	________
	________
Total number of housing units:	________

B **What other types of housing do you have in your town or city?**

C **What types of homes are in your town? Make groups of five or six students and complete the chart.**

What's your name?	What type of housing do you live in?

D **Now put the information into a pie chart. Look at the example on the left, then complete the chart on the right with your group's information.**

EXAMPLE:

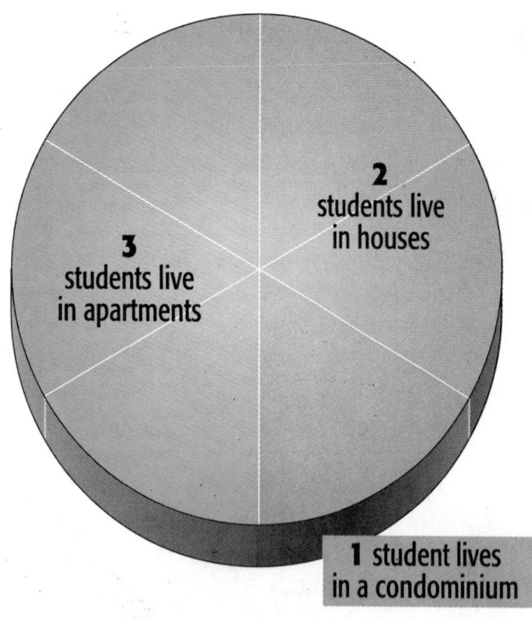

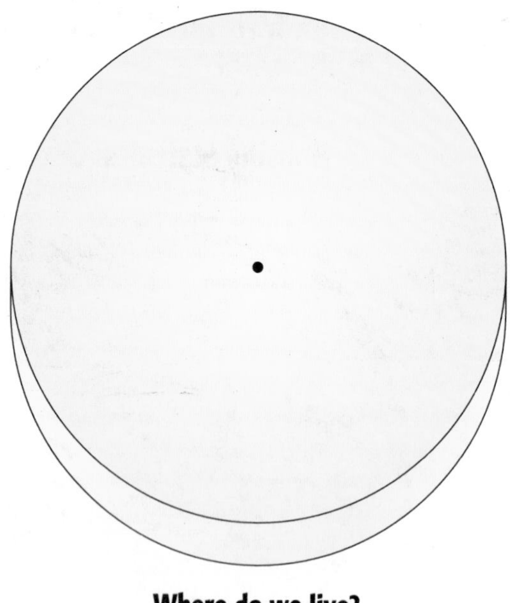

Where do we live?

E **Write two sentences about your group's pie chart.**

EXAMPLE: ***Two students in my group live in single-family houses.***

1. ______________________________

2. ______________________________

Describing your home

GOAL ▶ **Talk about rooms in a home** — *Vocabulary*

Listen to Saud and the real estate agent. How many bedrooms and bathrooms does Saud need? Then listen to the other conversations and fill in the information below.

Name	No. of bedrooms	No. of bathrooms
1. Saud		
2. Silvia		
3. Tien		
4. Felipe		

Where is Saud? Why is he there?

B **Where in the house do people do these things? With a group, write the names of the rooms. Use the words from the box.**

Activity	Room
People sleep in this room.	bedroom
People take showers in this room.	
People watch TV in this room.	
People eat dinner in this room.	
People make dinner in this room.	
People go from room to room here.	
People entertain in this room.	
People enter a home here.	
Children play outside here.	

bedroom	bathroom	yard	dining room	hall
kitchen	living room*	front door	family room*	

* Many people have one room and they call it both family room and living room.

C **Study the picture with your teacher. Write the correct letter next to each word.**

_____ garage	_____ swimming pool	_____ bathroom	_____ family room
_____ kitchen	_____ hall	_____ balcony	_____ front porch
_____ bedroom	_____ deck	_____ stairs	
_____ front yard	_____ back yard	_____ driveway	

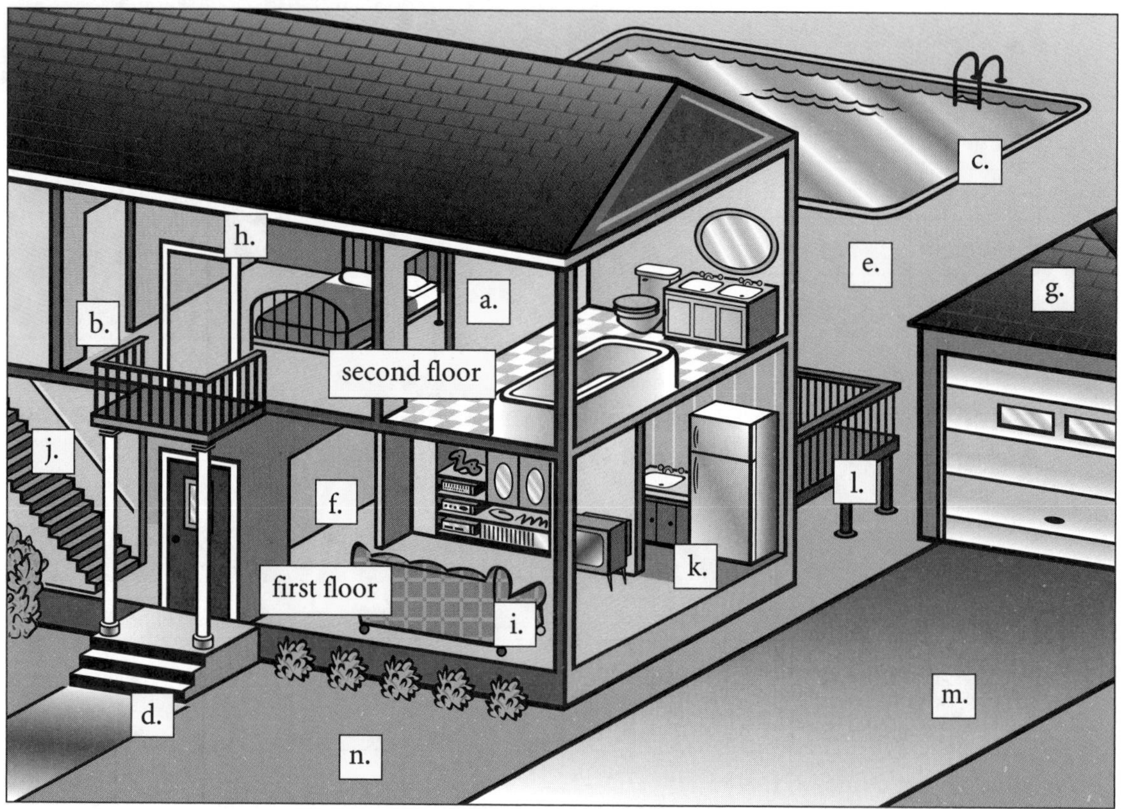

D **Ask your partner about his or her home.**

1. What kind of home do you have?
2. How many bedrooms do you have?
3. How many bathrooms do you have?
4. Do you have a front or back yard?
5. Do you have a garage or a carport?
6. Do you have a balcony?

carport

LESSON 3 Apartment for rent

GOAL ▶ Read and interpret classified ads | ***Life Skill***

A Read this ad from a newspaper.

APT FOR RENT

2 bed, 1 bath apt,
818 Sundry Ave. #19.
$750, furn a/c
all utls pd 1 mth dep.
call 555-7744

B Draw a line from the word to its abbreviation. What do these words mean?

apartment	utls
furnished	dep
utilities	apt
air conditioning	furn
paid	a/c
deposit	pd

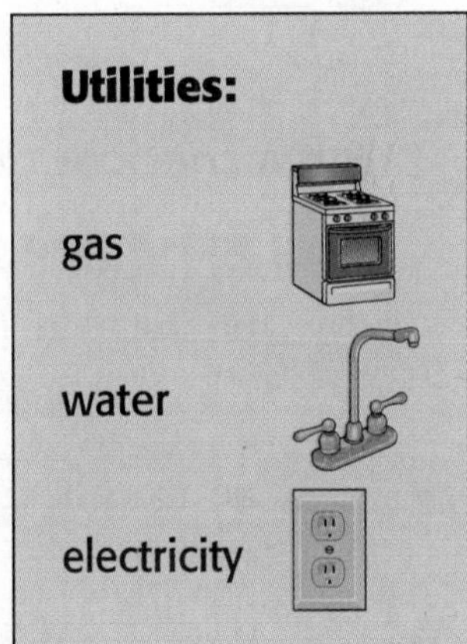

C Answer these questions about the ad in exercise A. Add one more question of your own.

1. Is it a house or an apartment? ____________
2. How many bedrooms does it have? ____________
3. Is it furnished or unfurnished? ____________
4. Does it have air conditioning? ____________
5. Are the utilities paid? ____________
6. How much is the rent? ____________
7. How much is the deposit? ____________
8. What's the address? ____________
9. What's the phone number? ____________
10. ____________?

GOAL ▶ Read and interpret classified ads — **Life Skill**

a.
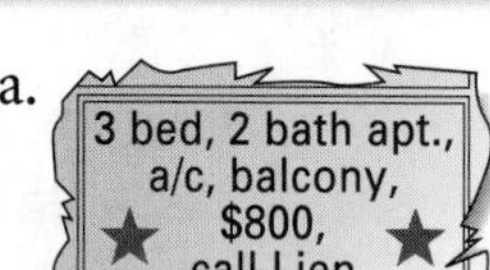
3 bed, 2 bath apt.,
a/c, balcony,
$800,
call Lien
at 555-7744

b.
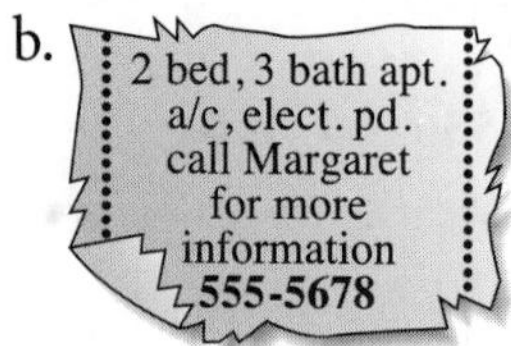
2 bed, 3 bath apt.
a/c, elect. pd.
call Margaret
for more
information
555-5678

c.

$700 a month.
1 bed, 1 bath apt.
n/pets. call Fred
at 555-7164

d.
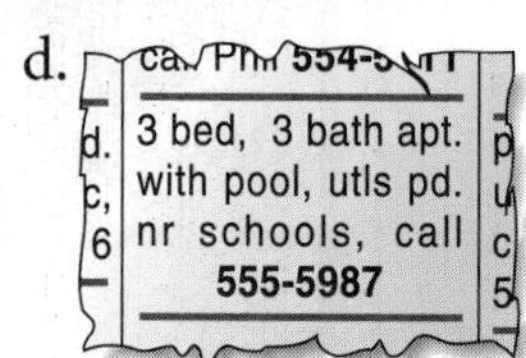
3 bed, 3 bath apt.
with pool, utls pd.
nr schools, call
555-5987

D **Listen and write the letter from the classified ads above.**

1. ____
2. ____
3. ____
4. ____

E **Put a check by things about your home.**

____ pets allowed

____ utilities paid (if you rent)

____ near a school

____ near public transportation

____ cable TV

____ air conditioning

____ near a park

____ garage

F **In a group, write a classified ad about your home.**

____

____

____

____

G **Active Task:** Go to a newspaper or look on the Internet and find a home to rent or buy that is good for your family.

LESSON 4 Making an appointment

GOAL ▶ **Use the present continuous** *Grammar*

What is Carmen doing?
Who is she talking to?

Listen to the conversation first with your book closed. Then read and listen.

Ms. Rollings: Hello.
Carmen: Hello. I am calling about the apartment for rent.
Ms. Rollings: Yes, it's still available.
Carmen: Can I see it?
Ms. Rollings: Of course, you can come to see it right now.
Carmen: I'm looking after my grandson right now. How about at 6 P.M?
Ms. Rollings: OK. What's your name?
Carmen: Carmen.
Ms. Rollings: See you at 6 P.M., Carmen.

With a partner, make new conversations using the information below.

Type of home	What are you doing?
house	I'm looking after my grandson.
apartment	I'm working.
condominium	I'm cleaning my house.
mobile home	I'm making dinner.

C Study the chart with your teacher.

Present continuous			
Subject	**be**	**Base + ing**	**Example sentence**
I	am	call + ing	I am calling about the apartment.
you	are	work + ing	You are working right now.
he, she, it	is	talk + ing	He is talking now.
we, they	are	look + ing	We are looking for a new house.

D Look at the pictures and write a sentence about each one.

1. eat

2. read

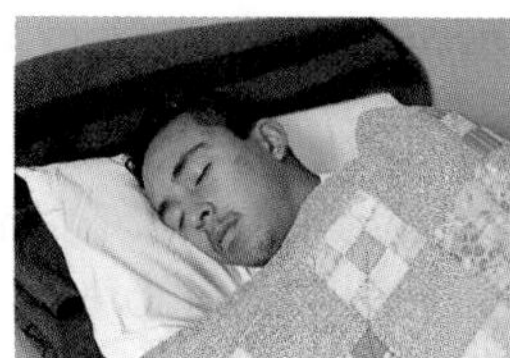
3. sleep

4. bark

1. ______________________
2. ______________________
3. ______________________
4. ______________________

E Write answers to the questions.

1. What are you doing right now?

____

2. What is your teacher doing right now?

____

3. What is your sister or brother or friend doing?

____

LESSON 5 Where do you put the refrigerator?

GOAL ▶ Use prepositions of location — *Grammar*

A **Write the words under the correct room. Tell your partner about your decisions.**

EXAMPLE: The bed goes in the bedroom.

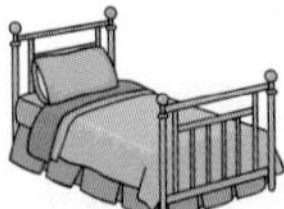

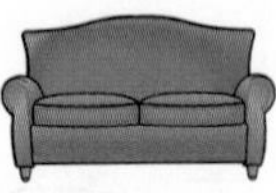

1. bed 2. car 3. chair 4. refrigerator 5. bathtub 6. sofa

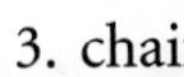

bedroom ____________

kitchen ____________

dining room ____________

bathroom ____________

garage ____________

living room ____________

B **In a group, make a list of other things you see in the rooms. Use a dictionary or ask your teacher for help.**

bedroom	kitchen	dining room	bathroom	garage	living room

C **Study the prepositions with your teacher.**

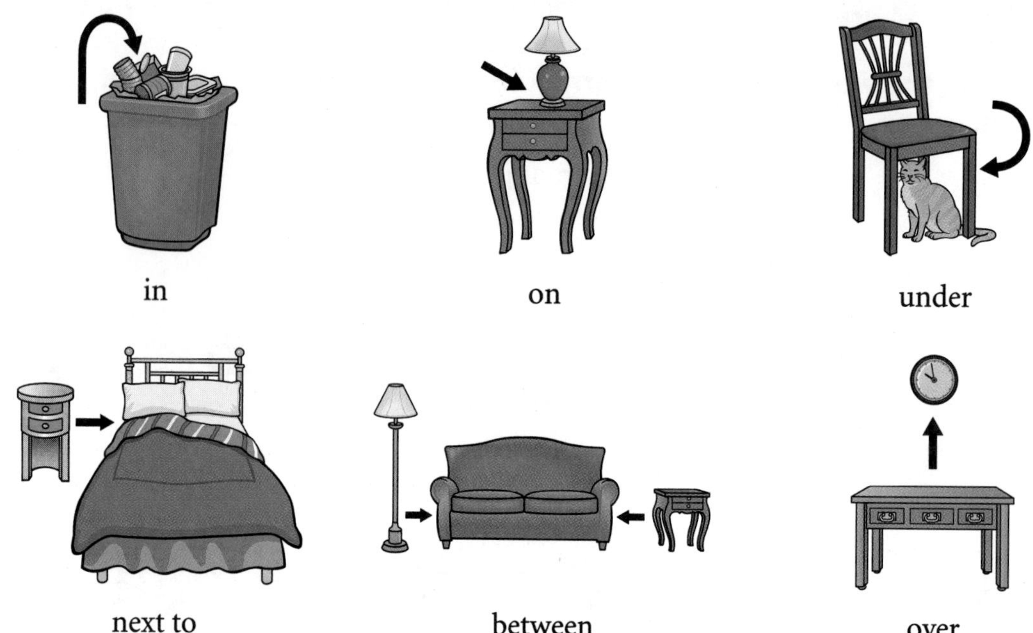

D **Ask a partner where things are. Ask about: the lamp, the cat, the nightstand, the sofa, and the clock.**

EXAMPLE:
Student A: Where's the trash?
Student B: It's in the trash can.

E **Use the prepositions above to identify the location of things in your classroom. Your partner will guess which thing you are talking about.**

EXAMPLE:
Student A: It's next to the window.
Student B: The TV.

Read and follow the directions below.

Below is a picture of a living room. Draw a window and a door. Put a painting on the wall. Put a sofa under the painting. Put a chair between the sofa and the door. Put a coffee table in the middle of the room. Draw an end table next to the chair in the corner. Put a lamp on the end table.

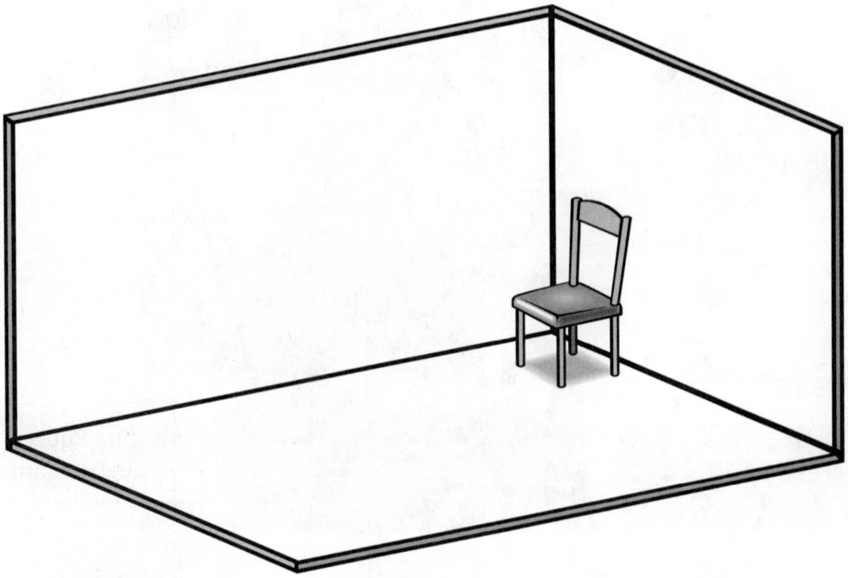

window  door  sofa  end table

coffee table  chair  painting  lamp

G Show your partner where the furniture is in your picture. Talk to your partner about it.

H Active Task: Find a picture of a room with furniture from a magazine or on the Internet. Show your picture to the class and describe it.

LESSON 6

Income and expenses

GOAL ▶ Understand a family budget

Life Skill

What are Roberto and Silvia talking about?

for rent: beautiful
3 bed, 2 bath hse,
nr schools, n/pets.
$1500 a month
call Marjorie at
555-4545

A Read about Silvia and Roberto.

Silvia and Roberto want to rent a new house, but it is very *expensive*. They need to *calculate* how much money they have. They also need to buy furniture for the house. Silvia and Roberto are making a family *budget* to see if they have *enough* money for a new house.

B What do the new words mean? Talk in a group. After you talk, ask your teacher. Try to make sentences with these new words.

expensive ______________________________

calculate ______________________________

budget ______________________________

enough ______________________________

C Look at Roberto and Silvia's income and expenses. What is their total income? What are their total monthly expenses if they rent the house for $1500?

income—money you earn
expenses—money you spend
savings—money you save
budget—money you plan to spend

	Monthly income	Monthly expenses
Roberto's wages	$1800	
Silvia's wages	$1070	
Rent		$1500
Gas		$ 50
Electric		$ 125
Water		$ 32
Insurance		$ 91
Credit card		$ 150
Savings		$ 200
Phone		$ 180
Food		$ 800
Roberto's ESL class		$ 74
Other		$ 100
Total income	$2870	
Total expenses		$3302

D Look at the words in the box. Talk about these words with your teacher.

income	expenses	budget	total	insurance	savings

E Silvia and Roberto need $432 more to rent the house. What can they do? Talk in groups.

F Do you have the same expenses? What other expenses do you have?

LESSON 7

Saving money

GOAL ▶ Make a family budget

Life Skill

Read about Roberto and Silvia's budget.

Roberto and Silvia want to rent a new house, but they don't have the money. They decide to make changes in their budget. One of the changes is to save money on their phone bill.

B Look at Roberto and Silvia's phone bill.

Southwest Phone Company				
Mar 06	9:32am	Mexico	20 minutes	$35.48
Mar 13	9:00am	Mexico	32 minutes	$56.22
Mar 20	9:17am	Mexico	29 minutes	$51.27
Mar 27	9:14am	Mexico	19 minutes	$33.75

C How much do they spend a month calling Mexico?

35.48
56.22
51.27
\+ 33.75
Total: ________

D How much is it if they talk only twenty minutes every week? How much do they save?

35.48
35.48
35.48
\+ 35.48
Total: ________
Savings: ________

Silvia and Roberto want to use their savings to rent a new house.
What do you want to use your savings for?

E **Look at the new budget. What is the new total without savings? How much money can they put into savings?**

	Monthly income	New monthly budget
Roberto's wages	$1800	
Silvia's wages	$1070	
Rent		$1500
Gas		$ 50
Electric		$ 100
Water		$ 32
Insurance		$ 91
Credit card		$ 120
Savings		
Phone		$ 145
Food		$ 550
Roberto's ESL class		$ 74
Other		$100
Total income	$2870	
Total expenses		

F **In groups, make a budget. There are five people in your family.**

	Income	Monthly expenses
Your family income	$3000	
Rent		
Gas		$ 50
Electric		$100
Water		$ 32
Food		
Life insurance		$ 91
Auto insurance		$200
Gasoline		
Phone		
Savings		
Other		
Total	$3000	

G **Report your budget to the class. How much is the rent?**

H **What are your other expenses?**

____

____

____

____

I **Active Task:** Make a real budget with your family.

Review

A **Read the classified ads.**

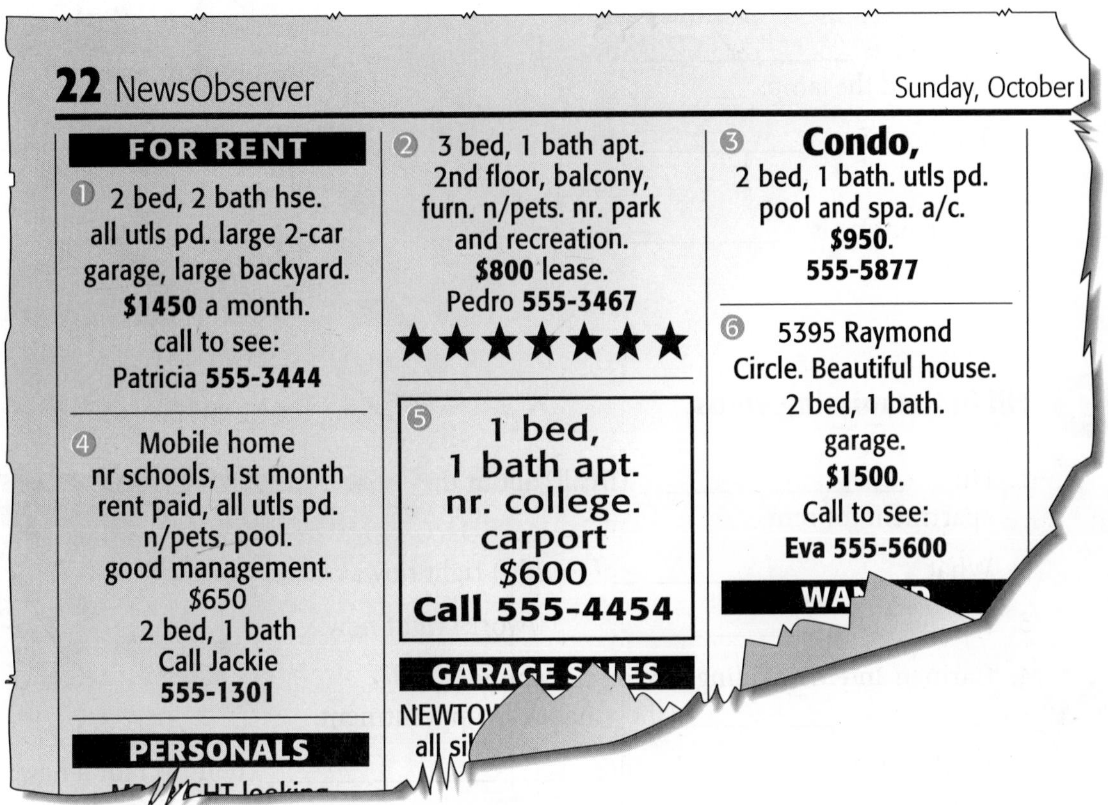

22 NewsObserver — Sunday, October 1

FOR RENT

1 2 bed, 2 bath hse. all utls pd. large 2-car garage, large backyard. **$1450** a month. call to see: Patricia **555-3444**

2 3 bed, 1 bath apt. 2nd floor, balcony, furn. n/pets. nr. park and recreation. **$800** lease. Pedro **555-3467**

3 **Condo,** 2 bed, 1 bath. utls pd. pool and spa. a/c. **$950**. **555-5877**

4 Mobile home nr schools, 1st month rent paid, all utls pd. n/pets, pool. good management. $650 2 bed, 1 bath Call Jackie **555-1301**

5 **1 bed, 1 bath apt. nr. college. carport $600 Call 555-4454**

6 5395 Raymond Circle. Beautiful house. 2 bed, 1 bath. garage. **$1500**. Call to see: **Eva 555-5600**

PERSONALS

GARAGE S…ES

NEWTO… all si…

WA…

B **Write the information from the ads in the chart below. Then ask your partner questions to check your answers.**

What type of housing is it?	How many bedrooms are there?	How many bathrooms are there?	Is it near anything?	How much is the rent?
1. *house*				
2.			park	
3.	2			
4.				
5.		*1*		
6.				*$1500*

C **Look at the picture and fill in the missing prepositions.**

1. The cat is ________________ the sofa.
2. The lamp is ________________ the sofa.
3. The sofa is ________________ the end table and the lamp.
4. The book is ________________ the end table.
5. The painting is ________________ the sofa.

D **Fill in the missing verbs.**

1. Hi! ______________________ (I/call) about the apartment for rent.
2. What ______________________ (you/do) right now?
3. I'm busy. ______________________ (I/work) right now.
4. Carmen and Ms. Rollings are on the phone. ______________________ (they/make) an appointment.
5. Saud is at the rental agent's office. ______________________ (he/look) for a new apartment.
6. We want a new house. ______________________ (we/read) the classified ads right now.

E **Write six words connected with making your budget.**

__________________ __________________ __________________

__________________ __________________ __________________

TEAM PROJECT

APT FOR RENT
2 bed, 1 bath apt,
818 Sundry Ave. #19.
$750, furn a/c
utls pd 1 mth dep.
555-7744

Planning a dream home

In this project you will make a floor plan of a dream house, make a classified ad for it, and present it to the class.

1. Form a team with four or five students.

   In your team, you need:

Position	Job	Student Name
Student 1 Leader	See that everyone speaks English. See that everyone participates.	
Student 2 Architect	Draw a floor plan with help from the team.	
Student 3 Decorator	Place furniture in the plan with help from the team.	
Student 4 Spokesperson	With help from the team, organize a presentation to give to the class.	

2. Choose a kind of home. Is it an apartment, house, condominium, or a mobile home?
3. Make a floor plan of the home.
4. Make a list of furniture for your home. (See pages 69 and 71.)
5. Decide where to put the furniture. (See page 71.)
6. Make a classified ad for your home. (See pages 65 and 66.)
7. Plan a presentation for the class and present your dream home.

PRONUNCIATION

Listen to these words. Underline the words which sound like *air*. Circle the words which sound like *ear*. Then listen again and repeat.

where	near	here	hair	year	wear	chair
hear	there	their	clear	stair	pair	tear

LEARNER LOG

Circle what you learned and write the page number where you learned it.

1. I can talk about types of housing.
   Yes Maybe No Page ______
2. I can talk about rooms in a home.
   Yes Maybe No Page ______
3. I can talk about things in a house.
   Yes Maybe No Page ______
4. I can understand classified ads.
   Yes Maybe No Page ______
5. I can use the present continuous.
   Yes Maybe No Page ______
6. I can use prepositions to describe location.
   Yes Maybe No Page ______
7. I can make a family budget.
   Yes Maybe No Page ______

Did you answer *No* to any questions? Review the information with a partner.

Rank what you like to do best from 1 to 6. 1 is your favorite activity. Your teacher will help you.

- ☐ practice listening
- ☐ practice speaking
- ☐ practice reading
- ☐ practice writing
- ☐ learn new words (vocabulary)
- ☐ learn grammar

In the next unit I want to practice more

________________________.

UNIT 5

Our Community

GOALS

- Identify places in the community
- Read city maps
- Give directions
- Use prepositions of location
- Identify public agencies and services
- Use the telephone
- Use simple present and present continuous

LESSON 1 Places in your neighborhood

GOAL ▶ Identify places in the community *Vocabulary*

A Look at the web page from the Internet with your teacher. Talk about the different sections.

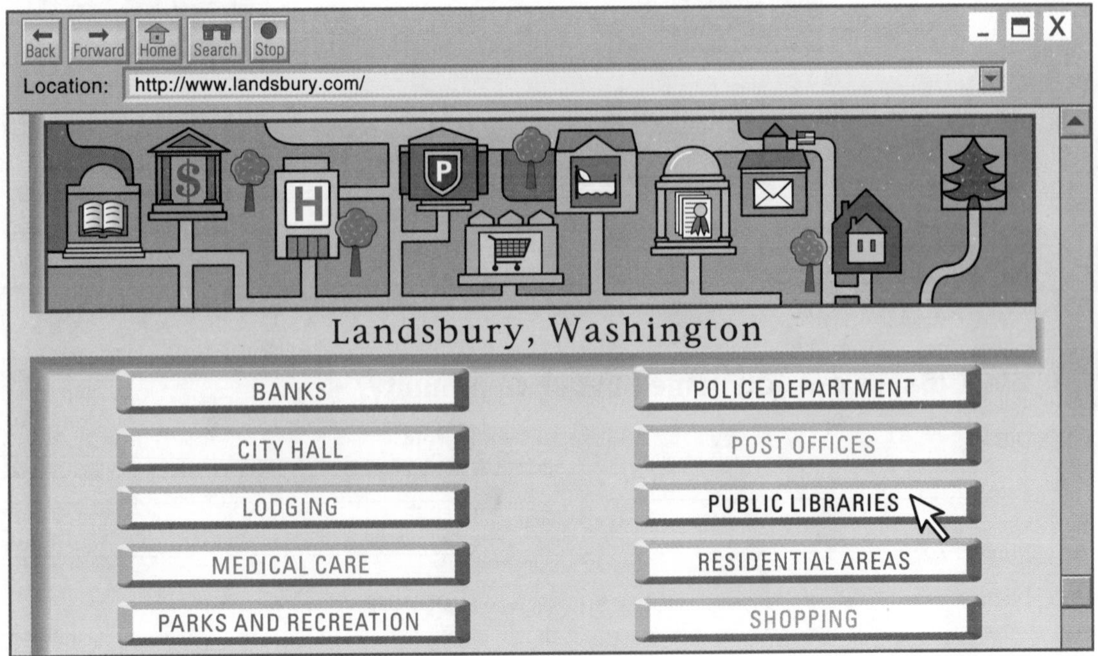

B Which of these are government offices?

C **Work in a group and put the words under the pictures.**

apartment	public pool	hotel	house
tennis courts	hospital	motel	playground
mobile home	doctor's office	dentist's office	hostel

Lodging

____
____
____

Medical care

____
____
____

Parks and recreation

____
____
____

Residential areas

apartment
____
____

D **What places can you name in your community?**

parks

____
____

hotels

____
____

banks

____
____

shopping centers

____
____

LESSON 2 Where's City Hall?

GOAL ▶ Read city maps — **Life Skill**

Where is Gabriela?
What is she doing?

A Practice the conversation.

Alma: Excuse me, I need to find City Hall.
Gabriela: Of course. Go straight ahead one block and turn right.
Alma: Straight ahead one block and turn right.
Gabriela: Yes. It's on the left.
Alma: Thanks.
Gabriela: No problem.

B Practice these words with the teacher.

left	right	straight ahead	block

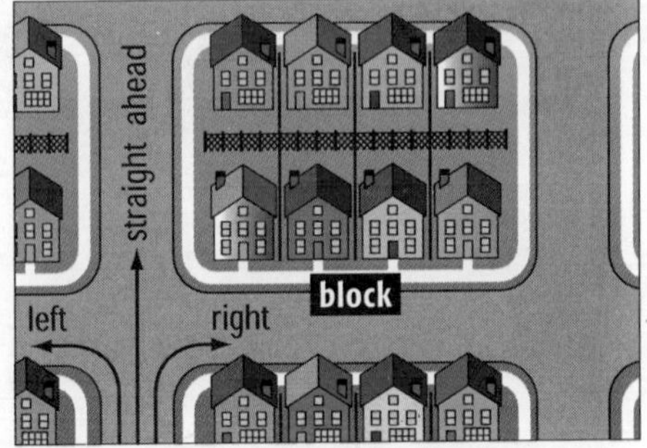

C With a partner, make new conversations. Follow the example in exercise A.

Place	Directions
City Hall	Go straight ahead one block and turn right. It's on the left.
Rosco's Buffet Restaurant	Go straight ahead two blocks and turn left. It's on the right.
the post office	Go straight ahead one block and turn right. Go one more block and turn left. It's on the right.
the zoo	Go straight ahead two blocks and turn right. It's on the right.
the high school	Go straight ahead two blocks and turn right. Go one more block and turn right. It's on the left.

D **Look at the map. You are in the car. Read the directions on page 83 and mark 1 to 5 in the squares on the map.**

1. City Hall
2. Rosco's Buffet Restaurant
3. the post office
4. the zoo
5. the high school

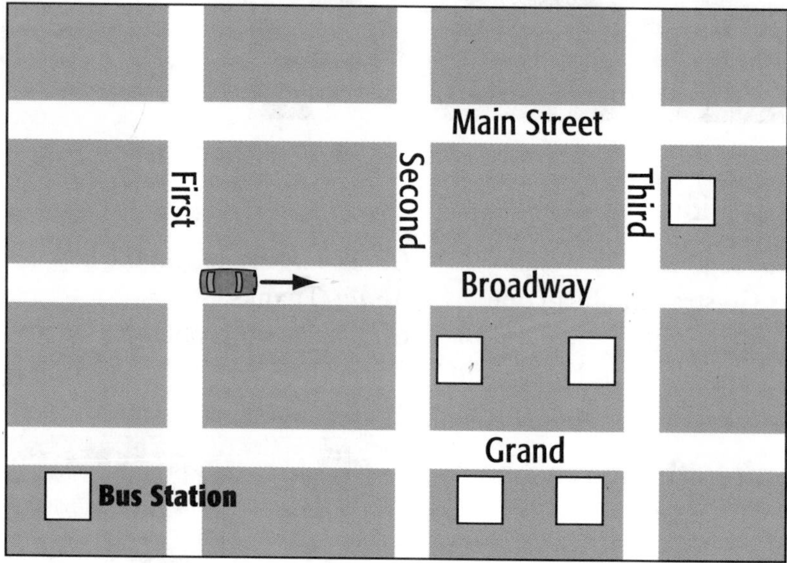

E **Where are the places? Complete the chart.**

Place	Location
Ex. the bus station	The bus station is on Grand.
City Hall	
Rosco's Buffet Restaurant	
the post office	
the zoo	
the high school	

F **Active Task:** Find a map of your city on the Internet or in a local bookstore. Find similar places in your neighborhood and tell the class where they are.

Finding the right place

GOAL ▶ Give directions — ***Life Skill***

A Write the words under the correct sign.

Turn around	Turn left	Go straight	Turn right

 ______

 ______

 ______

 ______

B Listen and check the box for the words that you hear.

	Turn right	Turn left	Turn around	Go straight
1. Directions to the mall.	x		x	
2. Directions to the post office.				
3. Directions to the movie theater.				
4. Directions to the museum.				
5. Directions to the park.				

C Ask four students where they live and fill in the chart below.

EXAMPLE:
Student A: Where do you live, Herman?
Student B: I live <u>in</u> Landsbury <u>on</u> Naple Avenue.

<u>in</u> the city
<u>on</u> the street

Student Name	City	Street
Ex. Herman	Landsbury	Naple Avenue
1.		
2.		
3.		
4.		

D **Draw a map from your school to your home.**

E **Practice giving directions to your home with three students. Use your map.**

EXAMPLE:
Student A: Can I visit you at your home?
Student B: Sure, come over any time.
Student A: Where do you live?
Student B: I live in Landsbury on Ludwig Avenue.
Student A: Can you give me directions?
Student B: Sure, look at the map. From the school, turn right on Snyder and left on Ludwig.
Student A: Thanks.

F **Listen to your partner's directions and draw a map to his or her home.**

G **Look at your map in exercise F and your partner's map in exercise D. Are they the same or different?**

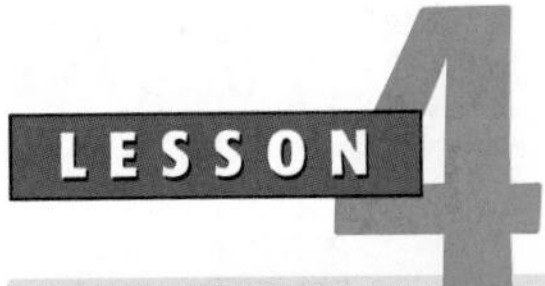

Is it next to the music store?

GOAL ▶ Use prepositions of location

Grammar

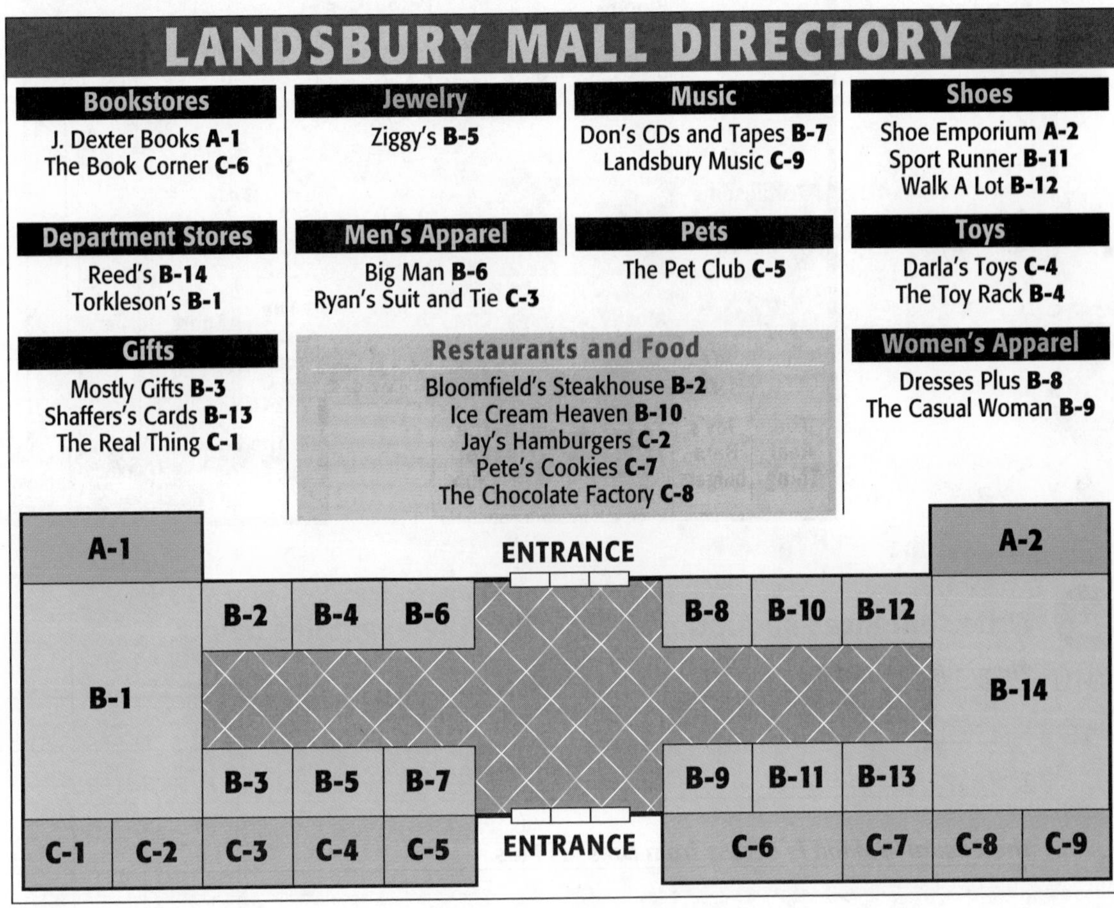

LANDSBURY MALL DIRECTORY

Bookstores	Jewelry	Music	Shoes
J. Dexter Books **A-1** The Book Corner **C-6**	Ziggy's **B-5**	Don's CDs and Tapes **B-7** Landsbury Music **C-9**	Shoe Emporium **A-2** Sport Runner **B-11** Walk A Lot **B-12**

Department Stores	Men's Apparel	Pets	Toys
Reed's **B-14** Torkleson's **B-1**	Big Man **B-6** Ryan's Suit and Tie **C-3**	The Pet Club **C-5**	Darla's Toys **C-4** The Toy Rack **B-4**

Gifts	Restaurants and Food	Women's Apparel
Mostly Gifts **B-3** Shaffers's Cards **B-13** The Real Thing **C-1**	Bloomfield's Steakhouse **B-2** Ice Cream Heaven **B-10** Jay's Hamburgers **C-2** Pete's Cookies **C-7** The Chocolate Factory **C-8**	Dresses Plus **B-8** The Casual Woman **B-9**

A **Answer the questions about the directory above.**

1. What store is next to Big Man? ______________________
2. What store is next to Dresses Plus? ______________________
3. What store is between The Pet Club and Ryan's Suit and Tie? ______________________
4. What store is between Landsbury Music and Pete's Cookies? ______________________

B **Scan the directory. Ask your partner.**

1. Where can you buy a dog? ***The Pet Club***
2. Where can you buy a suit for a man?
3. Where can you buy ice cream?
4. Where can you buy tennis shoes?
5. Where can you eat a steak?

C **Study the examples with your teacher.**

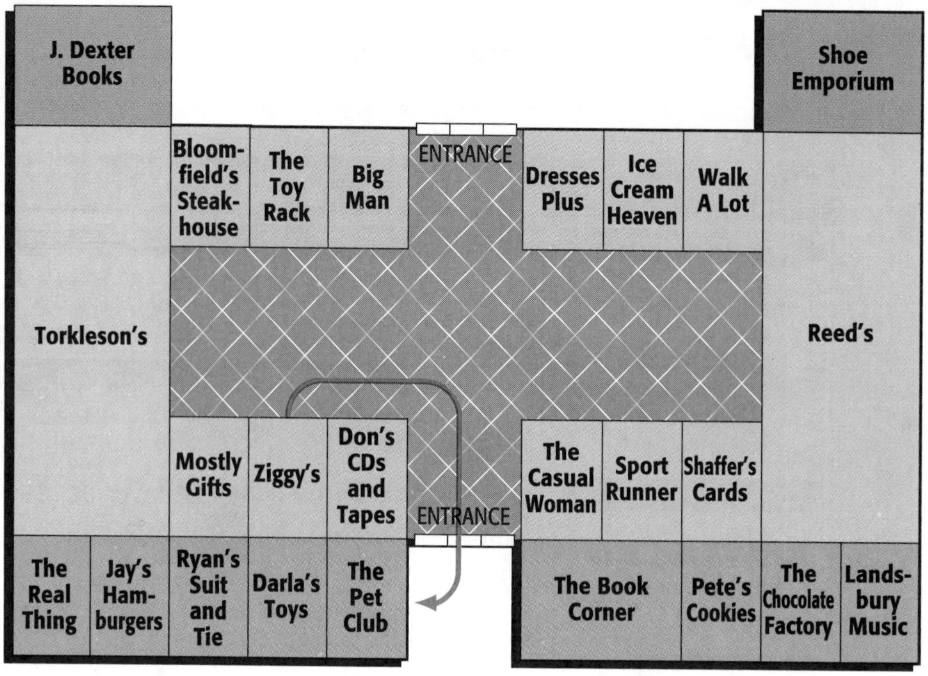

J. Dexter Books				ENTRANCE				Shoe Emporium
Torkleson's	Bloomfield's Steakhouse	The Toy Rack	Big Man		Dresses Plus	Ice Cream Heaven	Walk A Lot	Reed's
	Mostly Gifts	Ziggy's	Don's CDs and Tapes	ENTRANCE	The Casual Woman	Sport Runner	Shaffer's Cards	
The Real Thing / Jay's Hamburgers	Ryan's Suit and Tie	Darla's Toys	The Pet Club		The Book Corner	Pete's Cookies	The Chocolate Factory	Landsbury Music

D **Write sentences about the mall. Follow the examples below.**

Ziggy's is around the corner from the Pet Club.

1. ______________________________
2. ______________________________

The Casual Woman is across from Dresses Plus.

1. ______________________________
2. ______________________________

Landsbury Music is on the corner.

1. ______________________________
2. ______________________________

Sport Runner is between Shaffer's Cards and The Casual Woman.

1. ______________________________
2. ______________________________

The Book Corner is next to Pete's Cookies.

1. ______________________________
2. ______________________________

E **Practice the conversation.**

Student A: Excuse me. Can you help me?
Student B: Sure.
Student A: Where is The Toy Rack?
Student B: It's across from Ziggy's.

F **Student A, cover page 88 and repeat the conversation. Write the information on the directory. Student B, look at page 88 to answer.**

Where is Ice Cream Heaven?
Where is Shoe Emporium?
Where is The Pet Club?

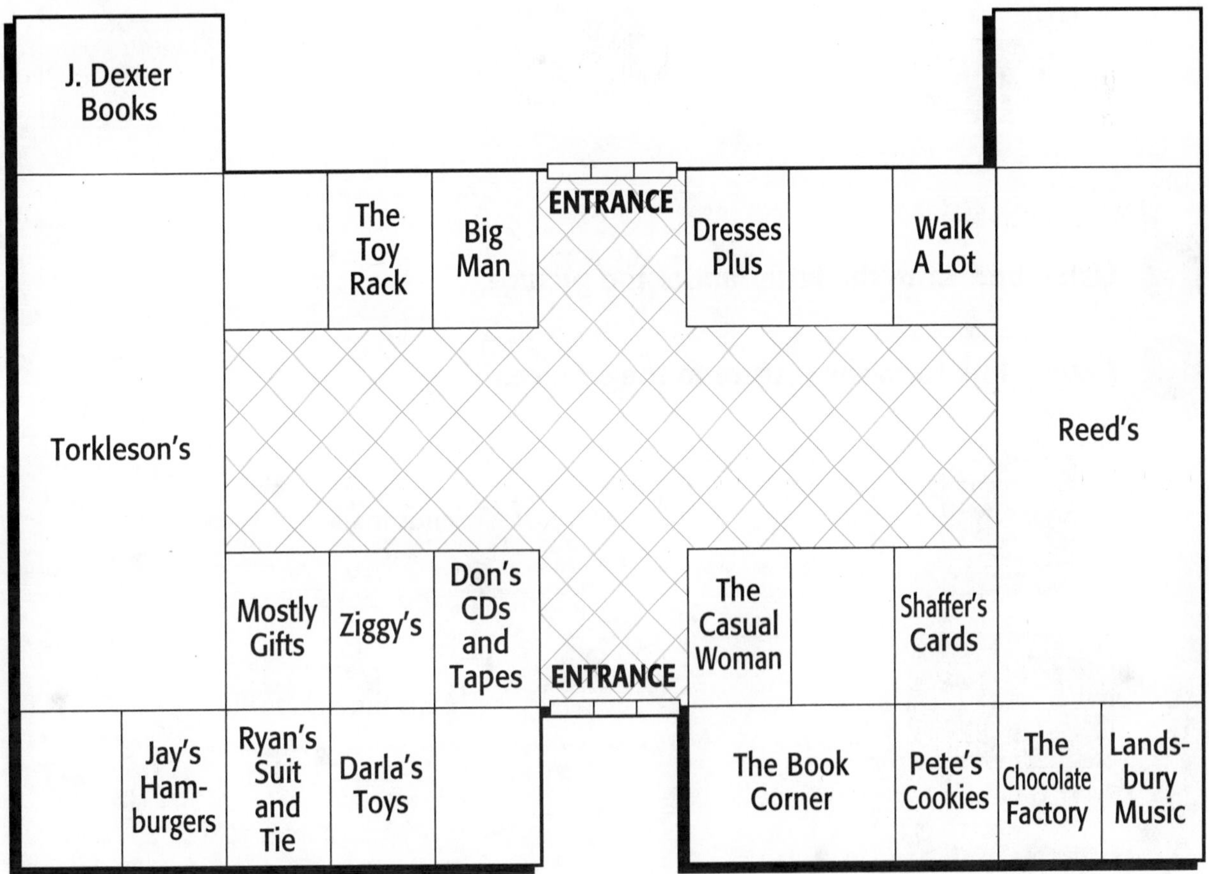

G **Student B, cover page 88 and repeat the conversation. Write the information on the directory. Student A, look at page 88 to answer.**

Where's Sport Runner?
Where's The Real Thing?
Where's Bloomfield's Steakhouse?

LESSON 5 Making a phone call

GOAL ▶ Identify public agencies and services — *Vocabulary*

A What are these places? Talk about the places with your teacher.

____ ____ ____

____ ____ ____

B Listen and write the letter under the picture.

C Draw a line from the picture to the service.

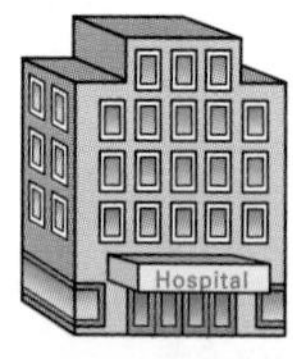

Sends mail.

Helps the sick.

Keeps your money safe.

Gives identifications and licenses.

What are they doing?
Who are they calling?

D **Listen to the conversation. Practice the conversation with new information.**

Emanuela: I need to call the hospital.
Lisa: Why?
Emanuela: My sister is very sick.
Lisa: The number is 555-7665.

Place	Problem
hospital	My sister is very sick.
bank	I need to see how much money I have.
DMV	I need a new license.
post office	The mail isn't here.

E **Make a bar graph of the class. How many students have been to these places in the United States?**

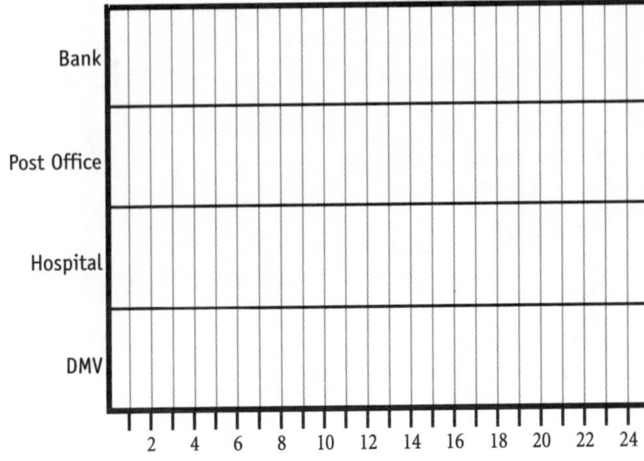

F **Active Task:** Find a telephone directory or go to the Yellow Pages on the Internet. Make a list of important numbers for you and put them by the phone.

LESSON 6 Leaving a message

GOAL ▶ Use the telephone — **Life Skill**

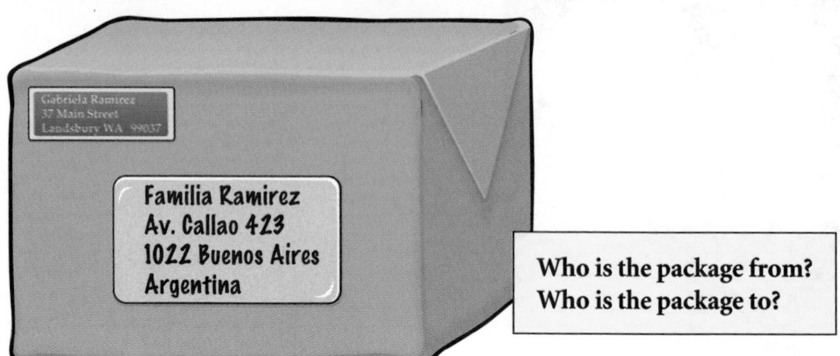

A **Read about Gabriela's problem.**

Gabriela needs to go to the post office. She wants to send a package to her family in Buenos Aires, Argentina. She doesn't know what to say at the post office.

B **Talk in a group. What can Gabriela do? Who can help her?**

She can ask ______________________________

She can call ______________________________

She can go ______________________________

C **Listen to Gabriela on the phone and answer the questions.**

1. Who does she talk to? ________________
   a. her friend David
   b. a machine
   c. David, her brother
2. When does she want to go to the post office? ________________
   a. today
   b. tomorrow
   c. Saturday

D **Look at the messages. Talk in a group. Circle three good messages.**

1. This is Gabriela. I need help. I want to send a package. Please call me at 543-2344. Thanks.
2. Call me. OK?
3. I am Gabriela. My phone number is 543-2344. Thanks.
4. This is your friend Gabriela from school. Can you help me? Thanks.
5. It is 3 P.M. on Friday. This is your friend Gabriela. My number is 543-2344. Please call me. I have a question for you. Thanks.
6. This is Gabriela. My number is 543-2344. I have a little problem. Can you call me back? Thanks.

E **There are three important parts of a message. Read the chart with your teacher.**

Your name	Reason for calling	Phone
This is Gabriela.	I have a question.	My number is 543-2344.
	I want to talk.	Call me at 543-2344.
	I need some information.	Can you call me back at 543-2344?

F **Practice leaving a message with two people. Student A writes the information he or she hears.**

EXAMPLE:
Student A: Hello, this is Gabriela. I can't come to the phone right now. Please leave a message.
Student B: This is Ramon. I have a question. My number is 543-2344.

Name: ____________________
Phone: ____________________
Reason for calling: ____________________
____

Name: ____________________
Phone: ____________________
Reason for calling: ____________________
____

LESSON 

Writing a letter

GOAL ▶ Use simple present and present continuous **Grammar**

A **Read Gabriela's letter to her family.**

January 24, 2003

Dear Mom and Dad,

I need to practice so I'm writing to you in English. I hope you understand. I am happy. I study English every day. I work at the market on First Street. I am a cashier.

Landsbury is a beautiful place. There are stores and restaurants. I sometimes eat at Bloomfield's Steakhouse in the Mall. The fire station is around the corner from my apartment. The bookstore is next to the fire station. My community is quiet. I am sending you a special map of the town with this letter.

I love you. Can you write me soon? I miss you.

Love,

Gabriela

B **Ask and answer with a partner.**

1. Where does Gabriela sometimes eat?
2. When does Gabriela study English?
3. Is Gabriela's community quiet or noisy?
4. Where does she work?

C **Answer the questions.**

1. Where do you like to eat? ______________________
2. When do you study English? ______________________
3. Is your community quiet or noisy? ______________________
4. Do you work? If yes, where do you work? ______________________

D **Study the charts with your teacher.**

Present continuous			
Subject	**be**	**Base + ing**	
I	am (I'm)	writing	right now.
he, she, it	is (she's)	walking	today.
you, we, they	are (they're)	reading	

100%		50%		0%
always	often	sometimes	rarely	never

Simple present		
Subject	**Verb**	**Example sentence**
I	study	I always study English.
he, she, it	works	She never works in a store.
you, we, they	eat	They sometimes eat steak.

E **Look at Gabriela's letter on page 94. Write all the present continuous sentences on a piece of paper.**

F **Look at Gabriela's letter from page 94. Write all the simple present sentences on a piece of paper.**

G **What are you doing right now? Write two sentences.**

1. ______________________________

2. ______________________________

Spelling note:
write–writing **sit–sitting**
drive–driving **hit–hitting**

H **Write a letter to a friend.**

Date: ______________________

Dear ______________________

I need to practice, so I'm writing to you in English. I hope you understand.

Your friend,

____

Review

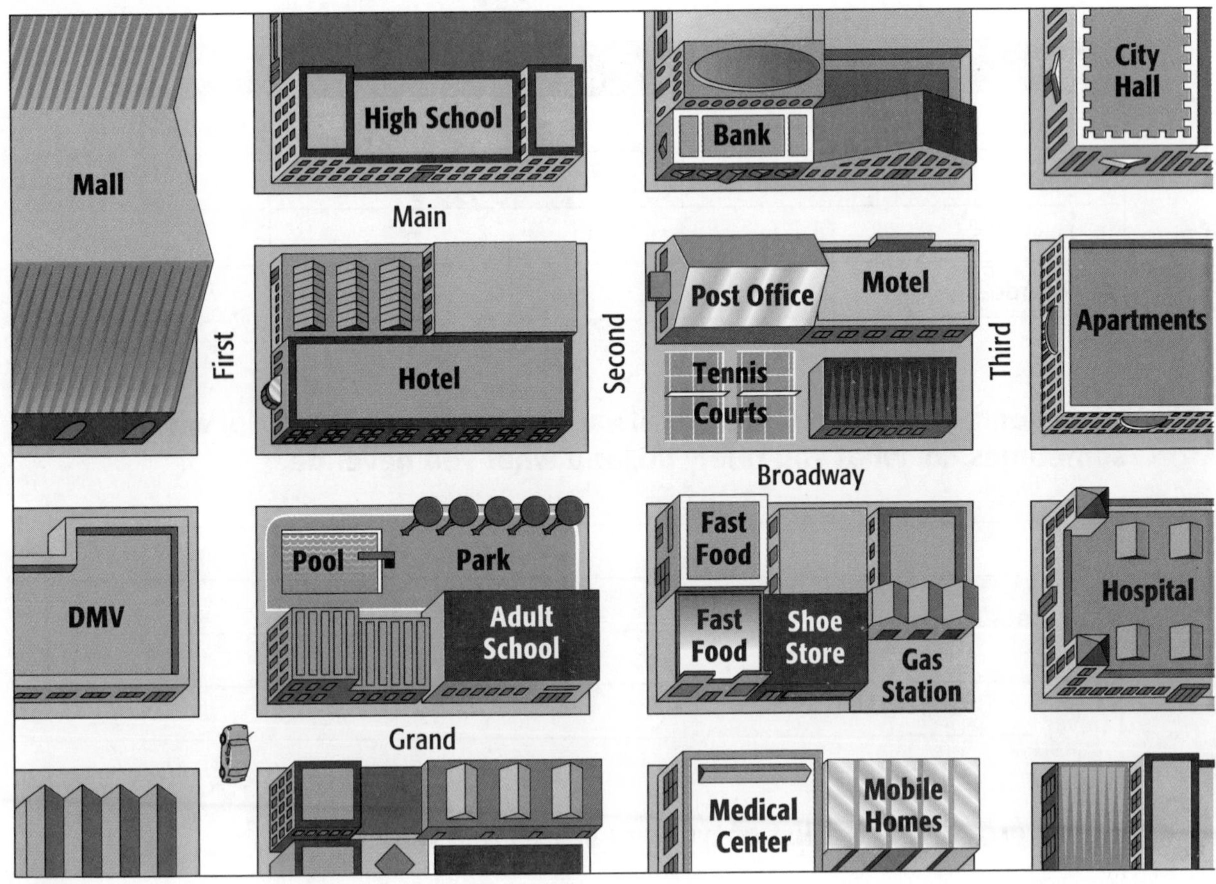

A Look at the map and ask a partner.

EXAMPLE:
Student A: Where are the tennis courts?
Student B: They are on Broadway, across from the fast-food restaurant.

Ask about these places:

motel	mobile homes	hospital
park	apartments	hotel
public pool	dentist	post office

B Give directions to a partner from the car to each location.

EXAMPLE:
Student A: Can you give me directions to the medical center?
Student B: *Yes, turn right on Grand. Go one block. It's on the right.*

hotel	apartments	City Hall
dentist	hospital	high school
bank	motel	DMV

C **Listen to the phone conversations. Complete the chart.**

Name	Reason for calling	Phone number
1. Nadia	I have a question.	555-2344
2. Vien		
3. David		
4. Ricardo		

D **Write sentences about what you always do, what you often do, what you sometimes do, what you rarely do, and what you never do.**

I always ______________________________

I often ______________________________

Sometimes I ______________________________

I rarely ______________________________

I never ______________________________

E **With a group, make a list of types of stores in a mall.**

______________ ______________ ______________

______________ ______________ ______________

______________ ______________ ______________

______________ ______________ ______________

TEAM PROJECT

Our new city

In this project you will make a brochure of a new city and present it to the class.

1. Form a team with four or five students.

   In your team, you need:

Position	Job	Student Name
Student 1 Leader	See that everyone speaks English. See that everyone participates.	
Student 2 City planner	Draw a map of your city with help from the team.	
Student 3 Designer	Make a brochure of your city with help from the team.	
Student 4 Spokesperson	With help from the team, organize a presentation to give to the class.	

2. Choose a name for your city.
3. Make a list of important places in your city and put them in alphabetical order. (See pages 81–82 for help.)
4. Make a map of your city and mark where the important places are. (See pages 84–85 and page 97 for help.)
5. Make a brochure. In the brochure put one paragraph about the city, the names of the team members, and a picture.
6. Prepare a presentation for the class.

PRONUNCIATION

These words all begin with /s/, together with another consonant. Listen and repeat.

study	station	straight	street	sport	special
school	skirt	slow	small	snow	swim

LEARNER LOG

Circle what you learned and write the page number where you learned it.

1. I can identify buildings.
   Yes Maybe No Page ______
2. I can read maps.
   Yes Maybe No Page ______
3. I can follow directions.
   Yes Maybe No Page ______
4. I can give directions.
   Yes Maybe No Page ______
5. I can read a directory.
   Yes Maybe No Page ______
6. I can use prepositions.
   Yes Maybe No Page ______
7. I can write a letter.
   Yes Maybe No Page ______
8. I can use the simple present and present continuous.
   Yes Maybe No Page ______

Did you answer *No* to any questions? Review the information with a partner.

Rank what you like to do best from 1 to 6. 1 is your favorite activity. Your teacher will help you.

- ☐ practice listening
- ☐ practice speaking
- ☐ practice reading
- ☐ practice writing
- ☐ learn new words (vocabulary)
- ☐ learn grammar

In the next unit I want to practice more

______________________________.

UNIT

6

Health and Fitness

GOALS

- **Identify body parts**
- **Identify symptoms and illnesses**
- **Use *should* for advice**
- **Read warning labels on medication**
- **Call 911 in an emergency**
- **Identify hospital vocabulary**
- **Use *want* plus infinitive**

LESSON 1 Parts of the body

GOAL ▶ Identify body parts *Vocabulary*

A Use the words from the boxes to label the pictures.

nose
mouth
head
tooth (teeth)
ear(s)
throat
eye(s)

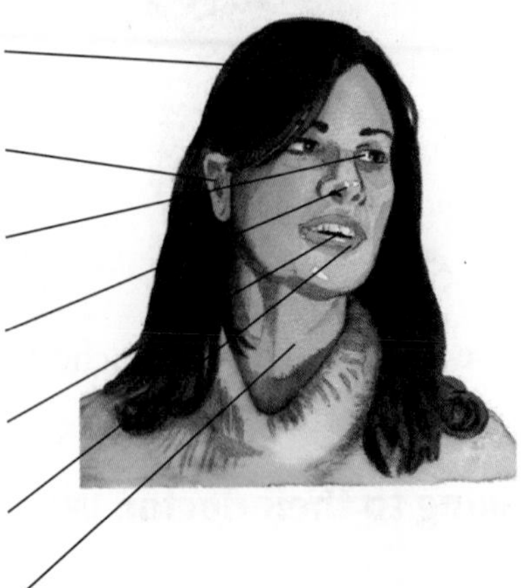

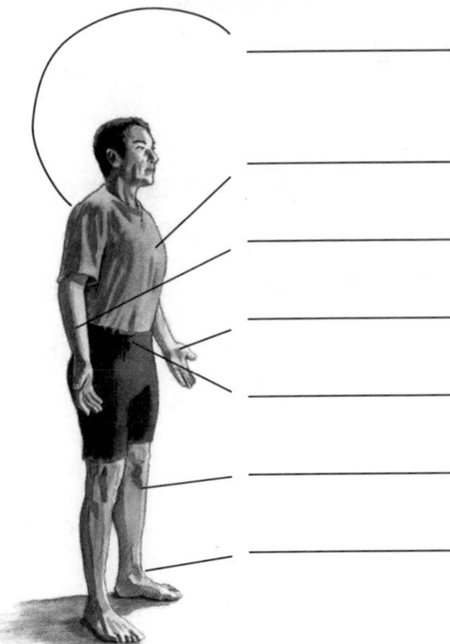

arm(s)	back	chest	leg(s)
stomach	hand(s)	foot (feet)	

> **I have** a headache / a stomachache / a toothache / a backache / an earache.
> My feet **hurt**. / My back **hurts**.

B Look at the pictures and complete the sentences.

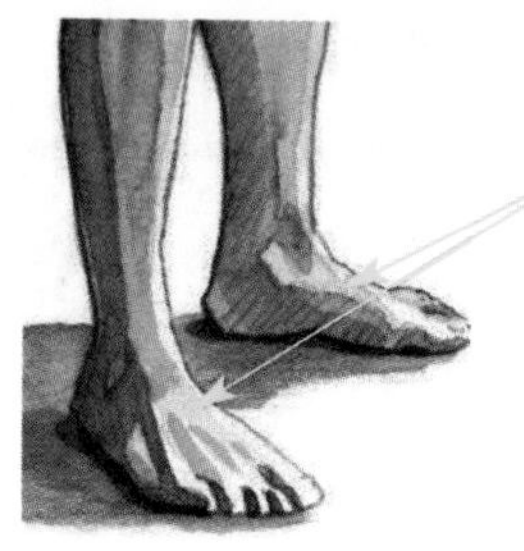

My ______________ hurt.

I have a ______________ ache.

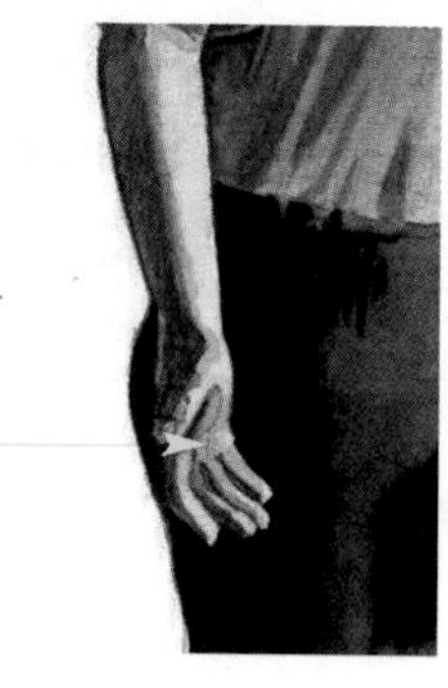

My ______________ hurts.

I have a ______________ ache.

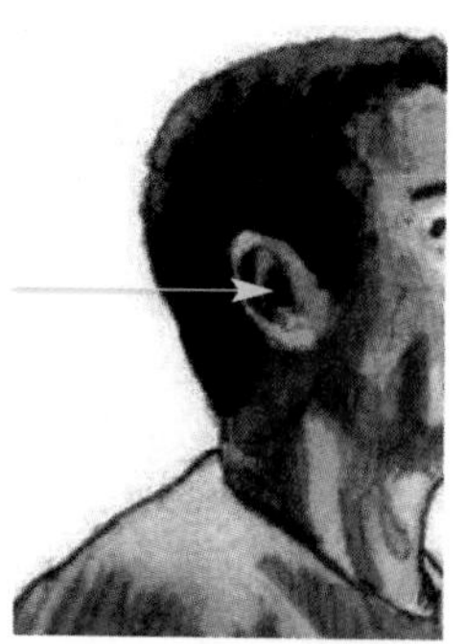

I have an ______________ ache.

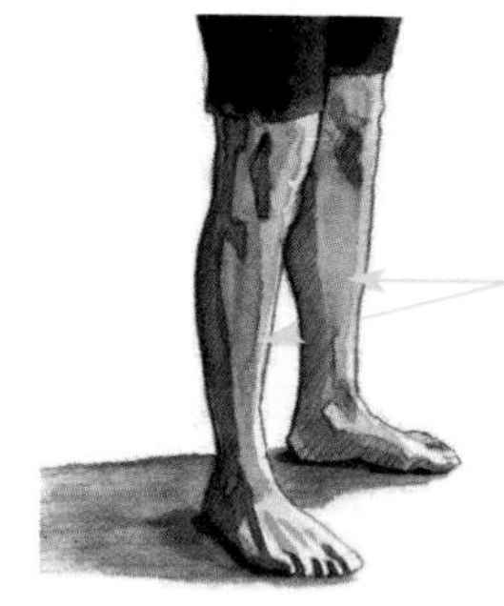

My ______________ hurt.

C Listen to these people talking to their doctor. What is the problem? Complete the sentences.

1. ***Karen:*** Doctor, my ______________ hurts.
2. ***Roberto:*** Doctor, my ______________ hurts.
3. ***Vien:*** Doctor, I have an ______________ ache.
4. ***Tino:*** Doctor, my ______________ hurt.
5. ***Eric:*** Doctor, I have a ______________ ache.

Is it a cold or the flu?

GOAL ▶ Identify symptoms and illnesses

Vocabulary

Label the picture with the words from the box.

runny nose
sore throat
fever
headache

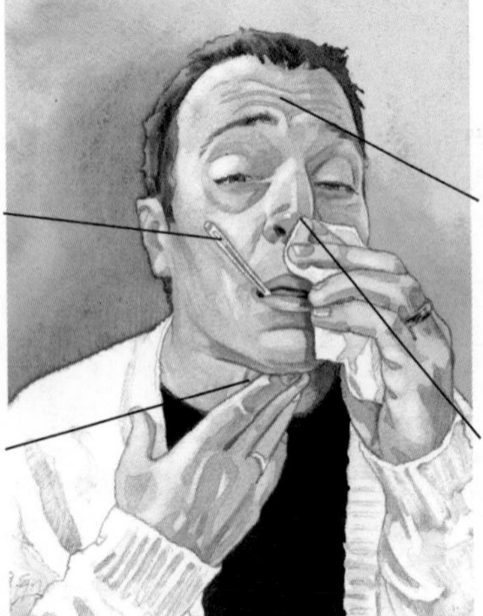

B **What is the matter with Eric? Does he have a cold or the flu? Read the paragraph and find out.**

Colds and the Flu

Colds and the flu are similar illnesses and have some of the same symptoms. The symptoms of a cold are a low fever, a sore throat, a headache, and a runny nose. People usually have a cold for one or two weeks. People with the flu feel very tired and sick. They often have a high fever, a dry cough, a headache, and muscle aches. People can have the flu for two to three weeks. Many people get colds or the flu every year and hate them both!

C **Answer the questions using the information from the paragraph.**

EXAMPLE:
People usually have the flu for ____________.
○ 1 week ○ 1–2 weeks ● 2–3 weeks

1. Colds and the flu are types of ____________.
   ○ symptoms ○ illnesses ○ medicines
2. Headaches and fevers are types of ____________.
   ○ symptoms ○ illnesses ○ medicines
3. When you have a cold, you ____________.
   ○ have a headache ○ have muscle aches ○ feel very tired
4. When you have the flu, you ____________.
   ○ have a low fever ○ feel very tired ○ have a runny nose

D **Complete the diagram using the information from page 103.**

Colds	Both	Flu
low fever	*headache*	________
________	________	________
________		________
________		________

I think you have **the** flu.
I think you have **a** cold.

E **Listen and complete the conversation.**

Doctor: What's the matter?

Miguel: Doctor, I feel very sick. I have a bad cough.

Doctor: Any other symptoms?

Miguel: I have a fever, too.

Doctor: ____

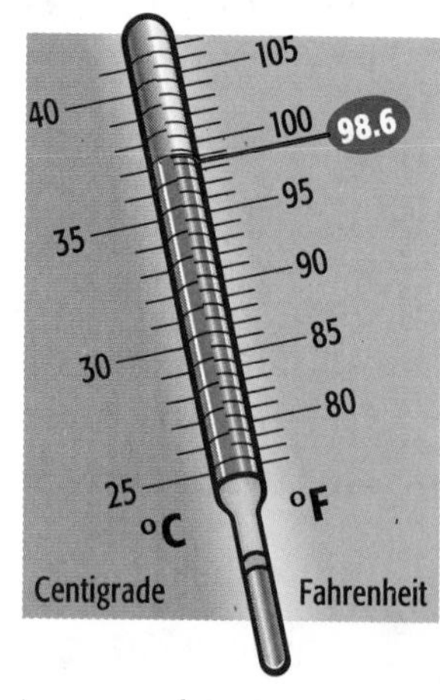

A normal temperature is ______ degrees.

F **Practice the conversation above. Use the symptoms from your diagram in exercise D.**

G **What other illnesses do you know? What are the symptoms?**

Illness	Symptoms
measles	red spots

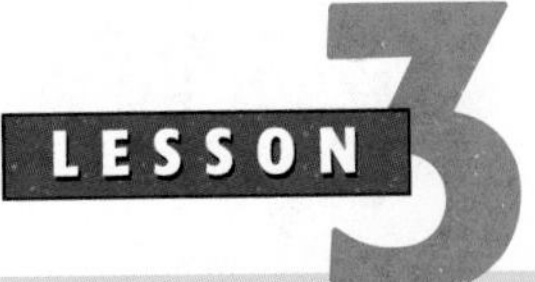

What should I do?

GOAL ▶ Use *should* for advice **Grammar**

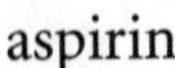

aspirin

cough syrup

throat lozenges

A **What do you usually do when you have these symptoms? Complete the chart.**

Symptoms	Take aspirin.	Rest in bed.	Take cough syrup.	Take throat lozenges.	Go to the doctor.	Other?
fever						
cough						
runny nose						
headache	x					x
sore throat						
stomachache						
backache						
feel tired						

B **What other remedies do you know for these symptoms?**

1. ______________________________
2. ______________________________
3. ______________________________
4. ______________________________
5. ______________________________

C **Study the charts with your teacher.**

Should			
Subject	***should***	**Base**	**Example sentence**
I, you, he, she, it, we, they	should	rest	He should rest.
		stay home	They should stay home.
		go to the doctor	You should go to the doctor.

Negative of *should*			
Subject	***should + not***	**Base**	**Example sentence**
I, you, he, she, it, we, they	should not (shouldn't)	go out	You should not go out.

Wh-* questions with *should				
Question word	***should***	**Subject**	**Base**	**Example sentence**
What	should	I, you, he, she, it, we, they	do	What should I do?

D **Ask and answer with five students. Use the symptoms from exercise A.**

EXAMPLE:
Student A: I have a headache. What should I do?
Student B: You should take some aspirin.
Student A: Thanks. That's a good idea!

Read the problem and give advice. Write one thing they *should* do and one thing they *shouldn't* do. Add two more problems of your own.

1. Roberto has a cold.

   He should take some cold medicine. He shouldn't drink cold drinks.

2. Phuong and Nam have the flu.

   They ______________________________

3. Michael has a sore throat.

   He ______________________________

4. Ayumi has a high fever.

   She ______________________________

5. Piedra has a backache.

   She ______________________________

6. Oscar feels very tired.

   He ______________________________

7. Tien is coughing a lot.

   She ______________________________

8. Omar has a stomachache.

   He ______________________________

9. ______________________________

   ____

10. ______________________________

    ____

Active Task: Find more information about cold and flu remedies at home or on the Internet. Bring the information to school to share with the class.

LESSON 4 Be careful.

GOAL ▶ Read warning labels on medication | **Life Skill**

What is Karen talking about?
What is the doctor writing?

A **Read about Karen.**

The doctor is giving Karen a prescription for some medicine. Karen is talking about the prescription with the doctor. The doctor is giving her instructions. The medicine is safe, but Karen needs to be careful.

B **Listen to the conversation between Karen and the doctor. What kind of instructions does the doctor give? Write the correct letter below each picture.**

___

___

___

___

GOAL ▶ Read warning labels on medication

Life Skill

Read the labels.

a.

b.

c.

d.

Warning:
Keep this drug and all drugs out of reach of children.
Follow directions carefully.
Don't take for more than 10 days.

D Answer the questions.

1. Look at the labels. Write what is the same on all the labels.

____

____

____

2. Write what is different on label a.

____

____

3. Write what is different on label b.

____

____

4. Write what is different on label c.

____

____

5. Write what is different on label d.

____

____

LESSON 5

Emergencies

GOAL ▶ **Call 911 in an emergency** — *Life Skill*

 **Talk about the pictures with your teacher.**

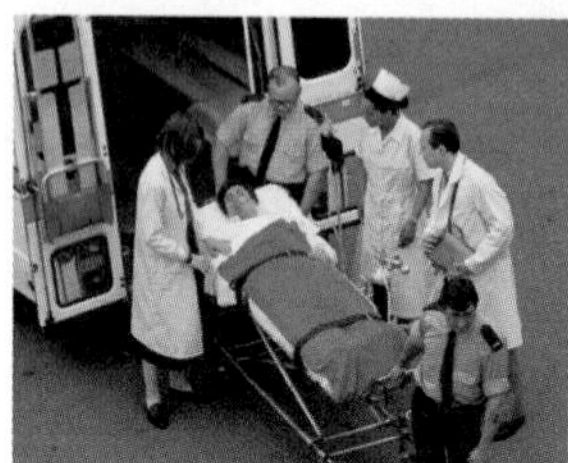
medical emergency

fire emergency

police emergency

Remember! You should only dial 911 when there is a fire or a medical or police emergency.

B **Talk about the problems with your teacher. Learn the new words and complete the chart in a group.**

Problem	Emergencies			Not an emergency
	Fire	Medical	Police	
Someone has a heart attack.		x		
Someone has the flu.				x
A house is on fire.				
Your car is stolen.				
Someone has a cold.				
Someone is hurt in a car accident.				
You need transportation.				
You see a robbery.				

  **Listen to these four conversations and circle the emergency.**

Who calls 911?	Type of emergency		
Ex. Rodrigo	robbery	car accident	(fire)
1. Anya	heart attack	fire	robbery
2. Felipe	car accident	fire	robbery
3. Brian	fire	robbery	heart attack

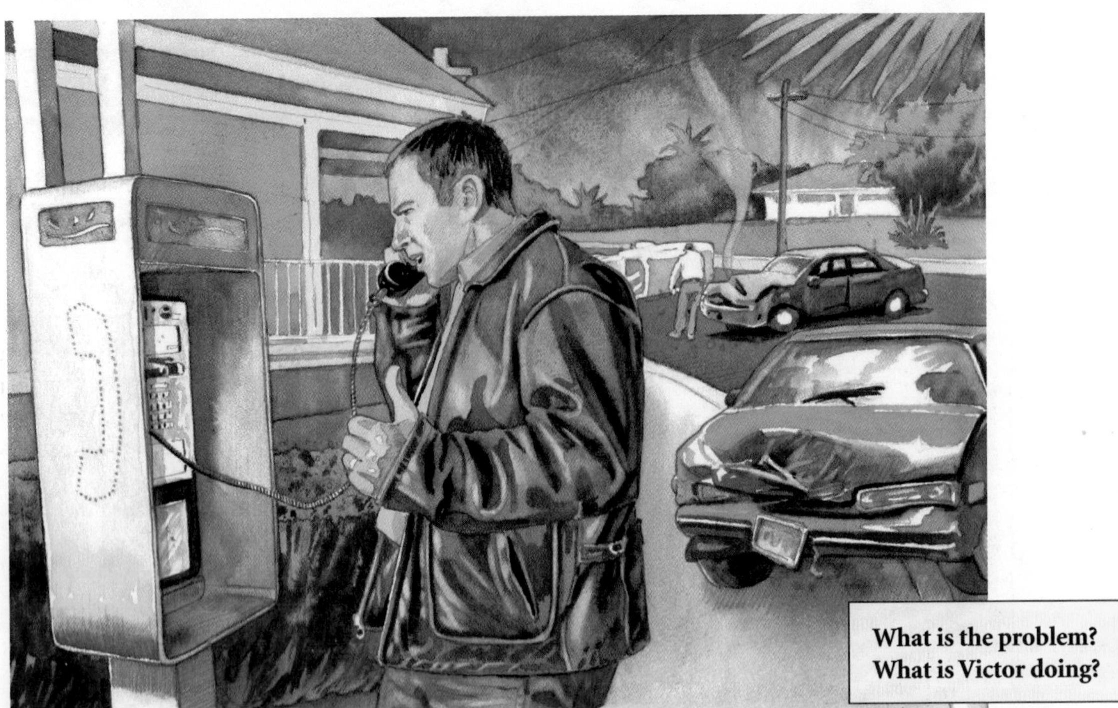

What is the problem?
What is Victor doing?

D Listen and practice the conversation.

Operator: 911. What is your emergency?
Victor: There's a car accident.
Operator: Where is the accident?
Victor: It's on Fourth and Bush in Santa Ana.
Operator: Is anyone hurt?
Victor: Yes.
Operator: What's your name?
Victor: It's Victor Karaskov.
Operator: OK, Victor, the police and ambulance are on the way.

E Answer the questions about the conversation.

1. **Who** is calling in the emergency? ______________________
2. **What** is the emergency? ______________________
3. **Where** is the emergency? ______________________

F With a partner, make a new conversation with one of the ideas.

Who	What	Where
Antonio	My father is having a heart attack.	Broadway and Nutwood.
Karen	There is a car accident.	First and Grand.
Tran	A house is on fire.	234 Jones Ave.

LESSON 6 Emergency room

GOAL ▶ Identify hospital vocabulary

Vocabulary

Townsen City Medical Center Directory

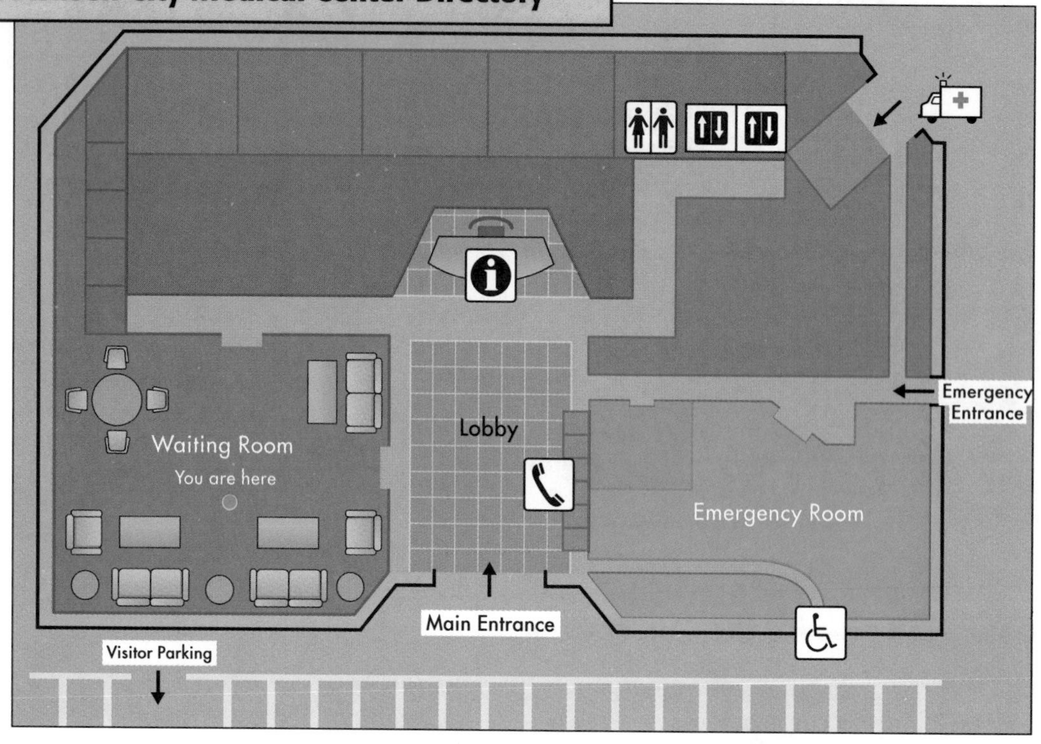

 ____  ____  ____

 ____  ____  ____

A Write the letter next to the correct symbol.

a. wheelchair entrance
b. restrooms
c. elevators
d. Information
e. pay phones
f. ambulance entrance

B Ask questions about places on the directory.

EXAMPLES:
Student A: Excuse me, where is Information?
Student B: It's over here. (Student B points to the map.)

Student B: Excuse me, where are the elevators?
Student A: They are over there. (Student A points to the map.)

C **Practice giving directions with a partner. You are in the waiting room.**

Student A: Excuse me, where are the elevators?
Student B: They are close to the restrooms.
Student A: Which way are they?
Student B: Go down the hall and turn left.

D **Ask about these places and make new conversations using the directory.**

the restrooms	the pay phones	the main entrance
the wheelchair entrance	Information	the main lobby

E **Make groups of four students. Prepare a short skit using words from this unit. Each person in your group will play one of these roles.**

Student A: You work in Information.
Student B: You are very sick.
Student C: You are a family member.
Student D: You are a nurse.

Some things you can say:	Some things the nurse can ask:
My son is very sick.	What's the matter?
We need a doctor.	What is your health insurance?
Where is the . . . ?	Are you pregnant?
I'm calling his wife.	Are you taking any medication?
We need a wheelchair.	Are you allergic to any medication?

F **Active Task:** Visit the main lobby of a hospital. Is there a floor directory? Write down three words you want to understand better.

LESSON 7 Staying healthy

GOAL ▶ Use *want* plus infinitive — **Grammar**

A **Read the information about exercise.**

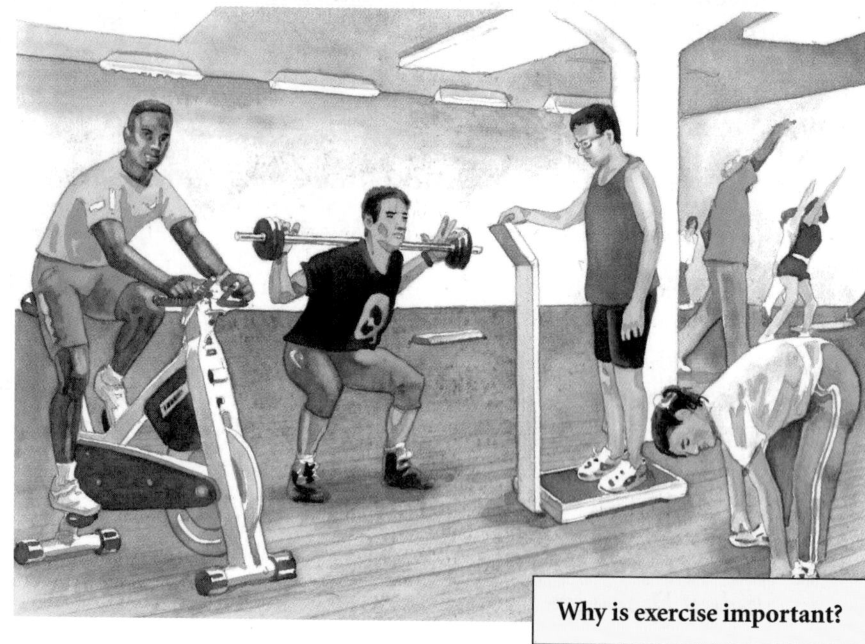

Why is exercise important?

Exercise

We need to exercise for many reasons. First, exercise is good for our hearts. Exercise builds muscles and makes us flexible. It is also good for our weight. Finally, when we exercise, we feel good. Exercise is very important for everybody.

B **Match the sentences and the pictures.**

_____ Exercise builds muscles.

_____ Exercise makes us flexible.

_____ Exercise is good for our weight.

_____ Exercise helps us feel good.

a.

b.

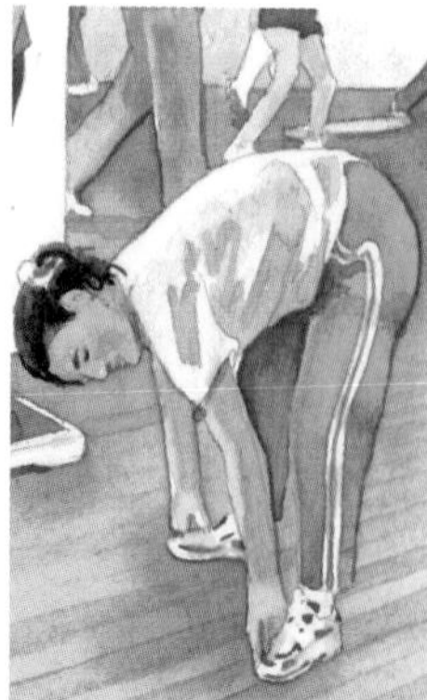

c.

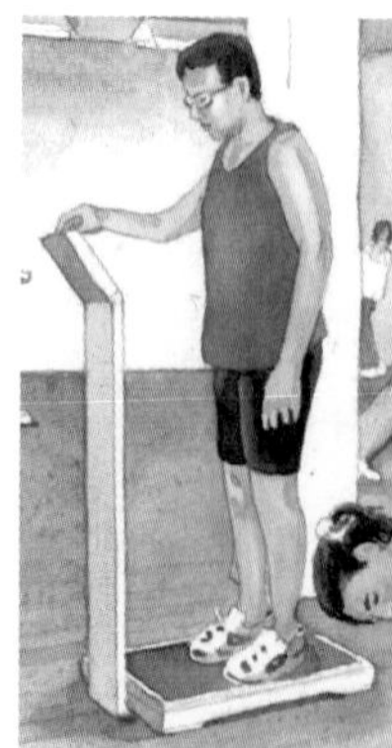

d.

C Talk about the pictures and read about exercise.

Exercise is important, but how much? Doctors say that 30 minutes a day is good. You can exercise at different times during the day. For example, try 10 minutes in the morning, 10 minutes at lunchtime, and 10 minutes at night. Running, swimming, housework, and yard work are all good exercise.

D Talk to three students and fill in the chart.

EXAMPLE:
Student A: How much do you exercise every week?
Student B: I exercise about 1 hour every week.

Name	0 minutes	Up to 1 hour	1–2 hours	2–3 hours	More than 3 hours
Ex. Karen			x		

E Write two or three exercise goals. How much do you want to exercise every week?

What exercise do you want to do?	When do you want to do this exercise?	How long do you want to do this exercise?
Ex. swim	8 A.M. on Saturday	40 minutes

F **Study the chart with your teacher.**

Subject	Verb	Infinitive (*to* + base)		Example sentence
I, you, we, they	want	to	exercise	I want to run.
he, she, it	wants		walk	We want to exercise.
			run	They want to walk.
			ride	He wants to ride a bike.
			do	She wants to go to the gym.
			go	

G **Write sentences about your goals from exercise E.**

EXAMPLE:
I want to run 20 minutes every day.

1. ______________________________
2. ______________________________
3. ______________________________

H **Ask three students about their exercise goals and write. Ask: What exercise do you want to do?**

EXAMPLE:
Karen wants to swim 40 minutes every day.

1. ______________________________
2. ______________________________
3. ______________________________
4. ______________________________
5. ______________________________
6. ______________________________

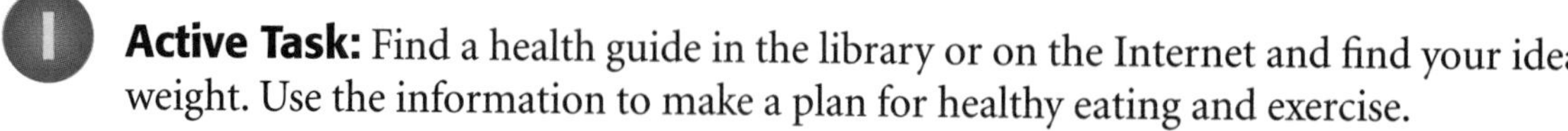

I **Active Task:** Find a health guide in the library or on the Internet and find your ideal weight. Use the information to make a plan for healthy eating and exercise.

Review

A **Look at the picture. Write the words.**

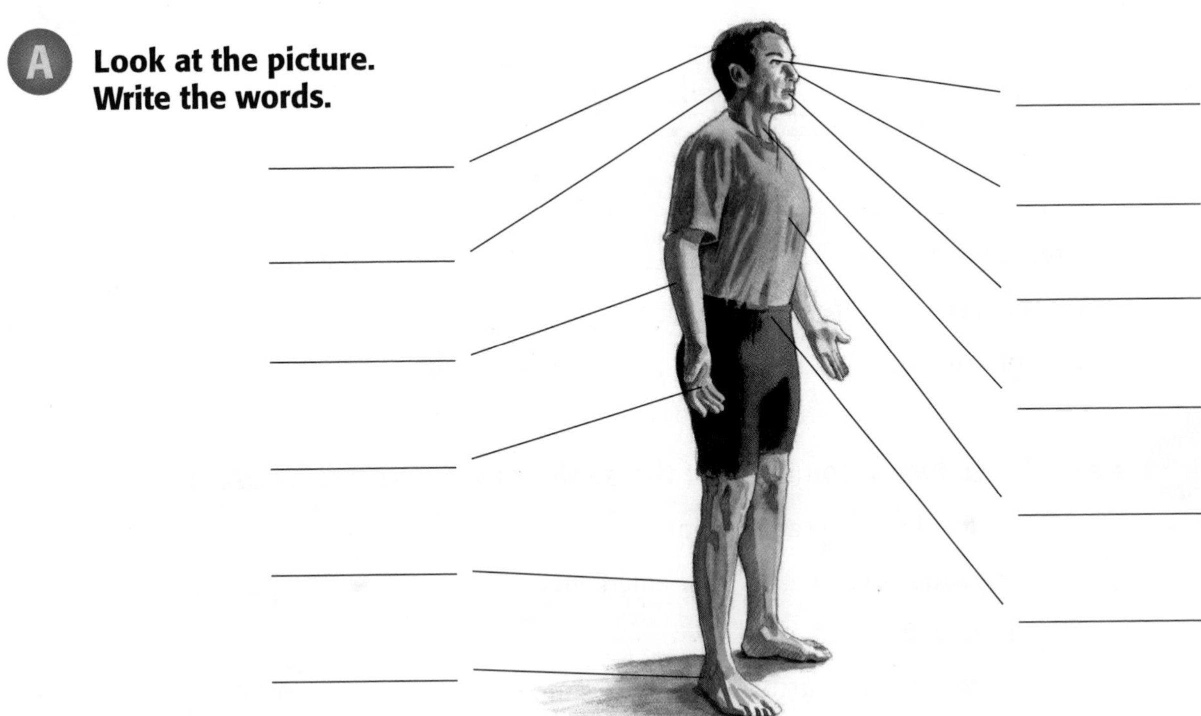

B **Match the symptoms and the remedy.**

____	1. fever	a. lozenges
____	2. backache	b. syrup
____	3. sore throat	c. rest
____	4. cough	d. aspirin

C **Practice the conversation with a partner. Make similar conversations using the words from exercise B.**

EXAMPLE:

Student A: What's the matter?

Student B: I have a ____________________. / My ____________________ hurt(s).

Student A: You should ____.

Student B: Thanks. That's a good idea.

D **You often find these warnings on medicine labels. Fill in the missing words.**

alcohol	reach	children	pregnant

1. Not for ______________________ under 12.
2. Keep this drug out of the ______________________ of children.
3. Do not take if you are ______________________.
4. Do not drink ______________________ with this drug.

E **Read the conversation and put the sentences in the correct order.**

_______ ***Victor:*** There's a car accident.

_______ ***Operator:*** 911. What is your emergency?

_______ ***Victor:*** Yes.

_______ ***Victor:*** It's on Fourth and Bush in Santa Ana.

___*5*___ ***Operator:*** Is anyone hurt?

_______ ***Operator:*** OK. The police and ambulance are on the way.

_______ ***Operator:*** Where is the accident?

F **Write six words you can see in a hospital.**

______________________ ______________________ ______________________

______________________ ______________________ ______________________

G **What kind of exercise do you do every day? How often?**

1. ____
2. ____

TEAM PROJECT

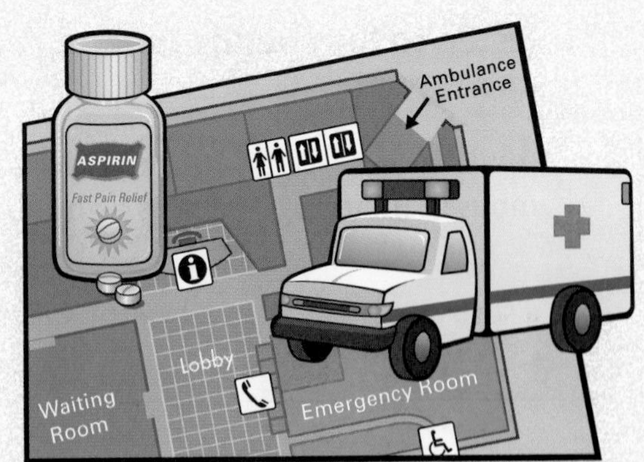

An emergency

In this project you will make a role play or a skit. Your group will perform the skit for the class. Members of your group will play the roles of: a patient, a family member, a 911 operator, an admitting person, a doctor.

1. Form a team with four or five students.

   In your team, you need:

Position	Job	Student Name
Student 1 Leader	See that everyone speaks English. See that everyone participates.	
Student 2 Secretary	Write out the skit and make parts for everyone with help from the team.	
Student 3 Director	Direct the skit.	
Student 4 Spokesperson	Introduce the skit.	

2. Choose an accident or illness. Write down the symptoms. Who is the patient in your group? What is his or her name in the skit? (See pages 103–106.)
3. Write a 911 call. Who is the operator? Who is the patient? Who is calling? Do you need to drive, or is an ambulance coming? (See page 111.)
4. Write a conversation with the doctor. Who is the doctor in your group? (See page 104.)
5. Write instructions and a warning for the medicine the doctor gives. (See pages 106–109.)
6. Practice the skit and present it to the class.

PRONUNCIATION

Listen to the sounds /s/ and /th/. Can you hear the difference? Listen and repeat.

think	sink	thick	sick	thigh	sigh	thumb	sum
mouse	mouth	moss	moth	mass	math	pass	path

a sore throat　　a healthy sport　　a thin slice　　three spoons

LEARNER LOG

Circle what you learned and write the page number where you learned it.

1. I can identify body parts.
   Yes　Maybe　No　Page ______
2. I can identify symptoms.
   Yes　Maybe　No　Page ______
3. I can use *should* to give advice.
   Yes　Maybe　No　Page ______
4. I can understand medicine labels.
   Yes　Maybe　No　Page ______
5. I can call 911.
   Yes　Maybe　No　Page ______
6. I can follow directions in a hospital.
   Yes　Maybe　No　Page ______
7. I can use *want to.*
   Yes　Maybe　No　Page ______
8. I can make exercise goals.
   Yes　Maybe　No　Page ______

Did you answer *No* to any questions? Review the information with a partner.

Rank what you like to do best from 1 to 6. 1 is your favorite activity. Your teacher will help you.

☐ practice listening

☐ practice speaking

☐ practice reading

☐ practice writing

☐ learn new words (vocabulary)

☐ learn grammar

In the next unit I want to practice more

______________________________.

UNIT

7

Working on It

GOALS

- Identify job titles
- Understand job vocabulary
- Use the simple past
- Prepare for a job interview
- Identify tools and skills for work
- Understand safety signs and warnings
- Use adjectives and adverbs

LESSON 1 What's your job?

GOAL ▶ Identify job titles **Vocabulary**

A **Write the job under the picture.**

teller	nurse	office worker	server	mechanic

Alan	Michelle	Isabel	Tony	Huong
			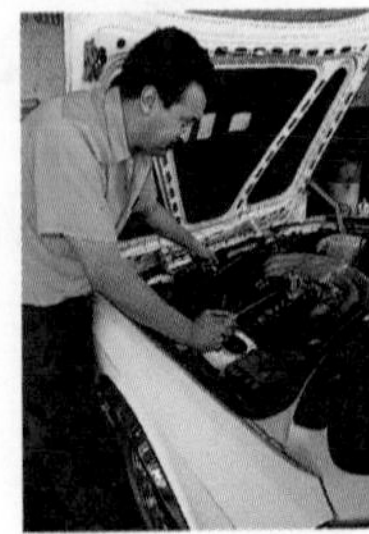	
________	________	________	________	________

B **In pairs, ask questions about each person.**

EXAMPLE:
Student A: What is Tony's job?
Student B: He is a mechanic.

C **Where do these people work? Complete the sentences using the words from the box. Then add one sentence of your own.**

restaurant	school	hospital	supermarket
office	bank	studio	garage

a nurse
an artist

EXAMPLE:
A nurse works in a hospital.

1. A mechanic ______________________.
2. An office worker ______________________.
3. A teller ______________________.
4. A server ______________________.
5. A cashier ______________________.
6. An artist ______________________.
7. A teacher ______________________.
8. ______________________.

D **Talk to four students.**

Name	What is your job?	Where do you work?
Ex. *Huong*	*nurse*	*hospital*
1.		
2.		
3.		
4.		

E **Make sentences about each student in exercise D.**

EXAMPLE:
Huong is a nurse. She works in a hospital.

1. ______________________.
2. ______________________.
3. ______________________.
4. ______________________.

LESSON 2 **Job hunting**

GOAL ▶ **Understand job vocabulary** *Vocabulary*

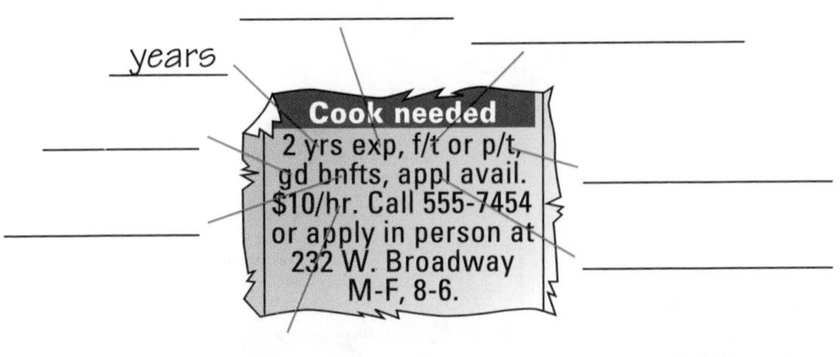

years
Cook needed
2 yrs exp, f/t or p/t,
gd bnfts, appl avail.
$10/hr. Call 555-7454
or apply in person at
232 W. Broadway
M-F, 8-6.

A Write the words with the abbreviations above.

~~years~~	experience	application	part-time
hour	good	full-time	benefits

B Listen to the conversations. Which benefits are they talking about? Fill in the circle next to the correct answer.

1. Listen to Roberto and his boss. Circle the benefit.
   ○ vacation ○ sick leave ○ insurance
2. Listen to Anya and her supervisor. Circle the benefit.
   ○ vacation ○ sick leave ○ insurance
3. Listen to Steve and his manager. Circle the benefit.
   ○ vacation ○ sick leave ○ insurance

What are benefits?

sick leave – you get paid if you are sick

insurance – you can get health insurance through your job

vacation – you get paid for a number of vacation days each year

C Read the advertisements.

1.

Nurse
f/t, gd bnfts,
2 yrs/exp necessary,
$22/hr.
call 555-3456

2.

Server
p/t, no exp nec.,
$5/hr. plus tips,
apply in person at
345 N. Witcomb Ave.
9am to 5pm, M-F

3.

★ Driver ★
f/t or p/t, work 7 days,
bnfts., $18/hr,
no exp, will train,
current driver's license,
speak Eng. and Span.
Call Emily at 555-5432

4.

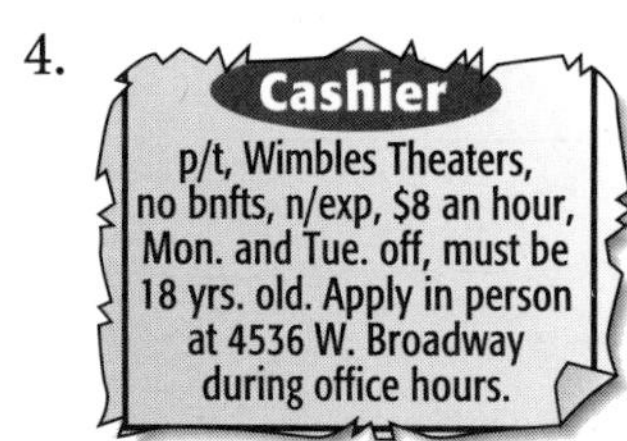

Cashier
p/t, Wimbles Theaters,
no bnfts, n/exp, $8 an hour,
Mon. and Tue. off, must be
18 yrs. old. Apply in person
at 4536 W. Broadway
during office hours.

5.

Mechanic
Mike's Garage,
f/t, night shift,
$12, bnfts, no exp,
will train.
Call 555-7469

D Complete the chart about the advertisements.

Position	Experience?	F/T or P/T	Benefits?	Pay
1.	2 years			
2. server				
3.		full-time and part-time		
4.			No	
5.				$12/hr

E Work in pairs. Ask and answer the questions about your job.

1. What do you do? ______________________
2. How many years of experience do you have? ______________________
3. Do you work full-time or part-time? ______________________
4. Do you have benefits? ______________________

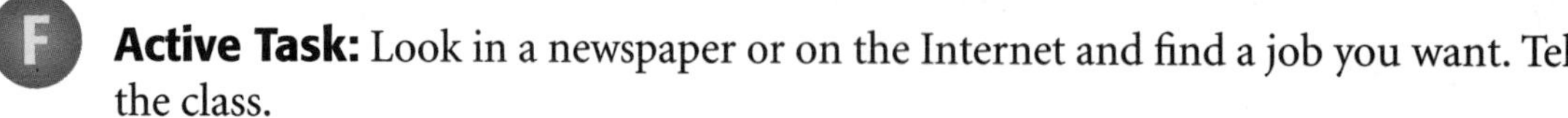

F **Active Task:** Look in a newspaper or on the Internet and find a job you want. Tell the class.

LESSON 3 What was your job before?

GOAL ▶ Use the simple past | **Grammar**

What is Francisco's job?
Does he work inside or outside?

A Read about Francisco.

My name is Francisco. I'm from Guatemala. Now I work in the United States. I'm a mail carrier. I deliver mail to about 200 houses every day. I started my job in July of 1999. Before I moved to the United States, I was a cook. I cooked hamburgers and French fries in a fast-food restaurant.

B Answer the questions.

1. Where is Francisco from? ______
2. What is his job now? ______
3. What does he do in his job? ______
4. When did he start his job? ______
5. What was his job in Guatemala? ______
6. Where did he work in Guatemala? ______

C Fill in the job history for Francisco.

Position	Company	From	To	Duties
Mail Carrier	U.S. Government			
Bus boy	La Cantina	03-1992	03-1995	Cleaned tables

D Study the chart with your teacher.

Simple past: Regular verbs			
Subject	**Base + *ed***		**Example sentence**
I	cleaned	tables	I cleaned tables.
you	cooked	hamburgers	You cooked hamburgers.
he	prepared	breakfast	He prepared breakfast.
she	delivered	packages	She delivered packages.
it	counted	the money	It counted the money.
we	helped	other workers	We helped other workers.
they	moved	to the United States	They moved to the United States.

Simple past: *be*			
Subject	***be***		**Example sentence**
I, he, she, it	was	a mail carrier	I was a mail carrier.
we, you, they	were	happy	You were happy.

E Write sentences about these workers.

EXAMPLE:
Anya was an office worker.
(type) She ***typed*** letters.

1. Ernesto was a delivery person.

   (deliver) He ____________________ packages.

2. David was a cashier.

   (count) He ____________________ money.

3. Anita was a nurse.

   (help) She ____________________ sick people.

4. Eva and Anya were teachers.

   (work) They ____________________ in a school.

F **Practice the conversation with your partner. Then make new conversations using the information below.**

EXAMPLE:
Miyuki: What was your last job?
Anya: I was an office worker.
Miyuki: What did you do as an office worker?
Anya: I typed letters.
Miyuki: What do you do now?
Anya: I'm a student. I study English.

	BEFORE	NOW
1.	cashier / count money	homemaker/look after my family
2.	teacher / help students	writer / write books
3.	mechanic / fix cars	driver / drive a taxi
4.	mail carrier / deliver letters	salesperson / sell computers
5.	cook / cook hamburgers	server / serve food
6.	busboy / clean tables	actor / make movies

G **Talk to four students. Ask them questions and fill in the chart.**

Name	What was your last job?	What did you do as a ________?
Ex. Francisco	I was a cook.	I cooked hamburgers.

LESSON 

A job interview

GOAL ▶ Prepare for a job interview

Life Skill

A **Look at the pictures. What is good in a job interview and what is not good?**

chewing gum

smoking

good posture

bright clothing

firm handshake

eye contact

B **Use the words above to complete the chart and add your own ideas.**

Good in a job interview	Not good in a job interview

Where is Miyuki?
What is she doing?

Read the conversations below. What is the next line in each conversation? Write the sentences from the box with the correct conversations. Then listen and check your answers.

Thanks. I'll wait here.	No, but I'm good at math and I learn quickly.
Can I make an appointment, please?	OK, can I have an application please?

1. ***Miyuki:*** Excuse me. I'm interested in a job. Do you have any openings?
   Manager: Not right now, but we can keep your name on file.

   Miyuki: ______________________________

2. ***Miyuki:*** Here is my application. Can I see the manager?
   Worker: Not just now, she's busy.

   Miyuki: ______________________________

3. ***Manager:*** Are you interested in a job as a clerk?
   Miyuki: Yes, that's right.
   Manager: Do you have any experience?

   Miyuki: ______________________________

4. ***Miyuki:*** I want to make an appointment to see the manager.
   Worker: Just a moment, I'll see if she's free.

   Miyuki: ______________________________

LESSON 5

Tools for work

GOAL ▶ Identify tools and skills for work

Vocabulary

A Talk about the tools with your teacher.

computer

saw and hammer

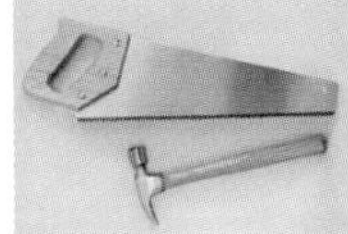

wrench

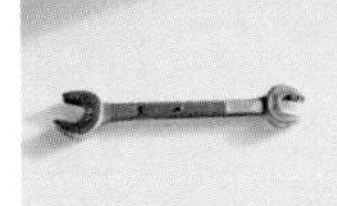

broom and mop

phone

copy machine

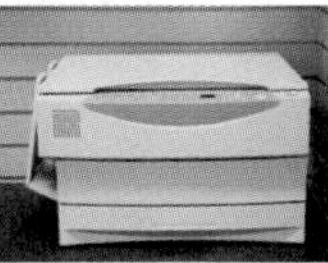

B Write one or two tools for each job.

Job	Tool	Skill
carpenter		
computer programmer		
construction worker		
custodian		
delivery person		
driver		
mechanic		
office worker		
student		
teacher		

C Look at the skills below. Complete the chart above with the skills from the box.

drives a truck	builds houses	delivers packages	writes programs
makes furniture	helps students	types letters	cleans offices
fixes cars	listens carefully		

Study the job history part of Ricardo's application.

can = ability
I can work.
You can sweep.
He can type.
She can drive.
We can help.
They can build.

Position	Company	From	To	Duties
Manager	The Happy Lunch Deli	9-18-99	present	managed 22 employees
Cashier	The Happy Lunch Deli	3-15-92	9-17-99	worked the cash register
Mechanic	Self-employed	7-2-83	3-14-86	fixed cars
Delivery Person	Mindanao Reporter	8-11-81	6-27-83	delivered newspapers

E What is Ricardo's experience? What can he do? Write sentences.

1. *Ricardo can manage 22 employees.*
2. *He can* ______________________
3. ______________________
4. ______________________

F What can you do? What tools can you use? Make a list.

Skills	Tools
I can	

G Active Task: Get a job application from a local business or from the Internet. What information does it ask for? Tell the class.

LESSON 6 Keep out!

GOAL ▶ Understand safety signs and warnings

Life Skill

1. 

2. 

3. 

4. 

5. 

6. 

A **Study the signs with your teacher. Write the warning words.**

Caution ____________________ ____________________

____________________ ____________________

____________________ ____________________

B **Listen to the description of a factory. Write the correct number next to each warning.**

_____ You must keep your hands away from this machine.

_____ You must watch your step when this area is wet.

_____ You must not smoke here.

__4__ You must wear a hard hat.

_____ You must keep this area clear.

_____ You must not enter.

C **Study the chart with your teacher.**

must				
Subject	***must***	**Base**		**Example sentence**
I, you, he, she, it, we, they	must	wear	head and eye protection	We must wear head and eye protection.
	must not	smoke	in this area	You must not smoke in this area.

D **Where can you see these warning signs, and what do they mean? Write one sentence for each sign using *must* or *must not*.**

EXAMPLES:
Danger No Entry ***You must not enter.***
Head protection required ***You must wear a hard hat.***

1. Keep out __________
2. No parking __________
3. Foot protection required __________
4. Go slow __________
5. Hot surface __________
6. Moving vehicles __________

E **Look in the classroom and in your school. What warnings can you say to another student?**

1. ***Be careful. You must*** __________
2. ***You must not*** __________
3. __________
4. __________

LESSON 

She's a very careful driver.

GOAL ▶ Use adjectives and adverbs

Grammar

A **Look at Fernando's evaluation. What is good? What is a problem?**

Evaluation Form

Date: May 4, 2003
Company: Paul's Radio and CD
Name: Fernando Gaspar
Position: Sales Clerk
Supervisor: Leticia Garcia

Punctuality:

(Needs improvement) Good Superior

Appearance (professional dress and grooming):

Needs improvement Good (Superior)

Communication Skills:

Needs improvement (Good) Superior

Product knowledge:

Needs improvement (Good) Superior

Comments:

Fernando is a good employee. I worked with him for eight hours today. He talked with the customers well. He was 10 minutes late to work. This is a problem. He says he has problems with his car. Fernando is a good salesperson and has a very good knowledge of the product.

Signed:

Leticia Garcia

B **Look at the evaluation. Answer the questions.**

1. Where does Fernando work? ______________________
2. What is his supervisor's name? ______________________
3. What does Fernando do well? ______________________
4. What does he do very well? ______________________
5. What does he need to improve? ______________________

C Study the chart and read the examples with your teacher.

Adjective	Example sentence	Adverb	Example sentence
good	I am a good speaker.	well	I speak well.
bad		badly	
slow	He is a slow driver.	slowly	He drives slowly.
quick		quickly	
loud		loudly	
quiet		quietly	
careful	They are careful workers.	carefully	They work carefully.

D Read the sentences and underline the correct word.

> **An *adjective* goes before a noun.**
> **An *adverb* goes after a verb.**

EXAMPLE:
He speaks English good/<u>well</u>.

1. She wears nice clothes to work. She always dresses good/well.
2. He speaks quiet/quietly, and I can't hear.
3. Anya can type very quick/quickly.
4. Rigoberto is a careful/carefully driver.
5. I don't have any experience, but I can learn quick/quickly.
6. Anya is a teacher, but she doesn't speak very loud/loudly.
7. A cashier counts money very careful/carefully.
8. Fernando is a good/well salesperson.

E Ask your partner. Use the words below.

EXAMPLE:
Student A: Do you drive slowly?
Student B: Yes, I do. / No, I don't. I drive quickly.

1. drive/carefully
2. cook/well
3. speak/loudly
4. type/quickly

Evaluation Form

Date: May 2, 2003
Company: Paul's Radio and CD
Name: John Perkins
Position: Sales Clerk
Supervisor: Leticia Garcia

Punctuality:

Needs improvement | (Good) | Superior

Appearance (professional dress and grooming):

(Needs improvement) | Good | Superior

Communication Skills:

Needs improvement | Good | (Superior)

Product knowledge:

(Needs improvement) | Good | Superior

Comments:

I worked with John for 4 hours. He is new. He needs to learn more about the product. He does not dress well and he needs to comb his hair. He says he was tired today. I think he has three jobs. This is a problem. John communicates well with the customers.

Signed:

Leticia Garcia

F **Read John's evaluation and answer the questions in a group.**

1. What does John do well?
2. What does he do badly?
3. Who is the better employee, Fernando or John? Why?

G **Talk to your partner. In your opinion, what makes a good employee? And what makes a good supervisor?**

Review

A **Write the name of the job below each picture.**

______________ ______________ ______________

B **Read the ads and complete the chart.**

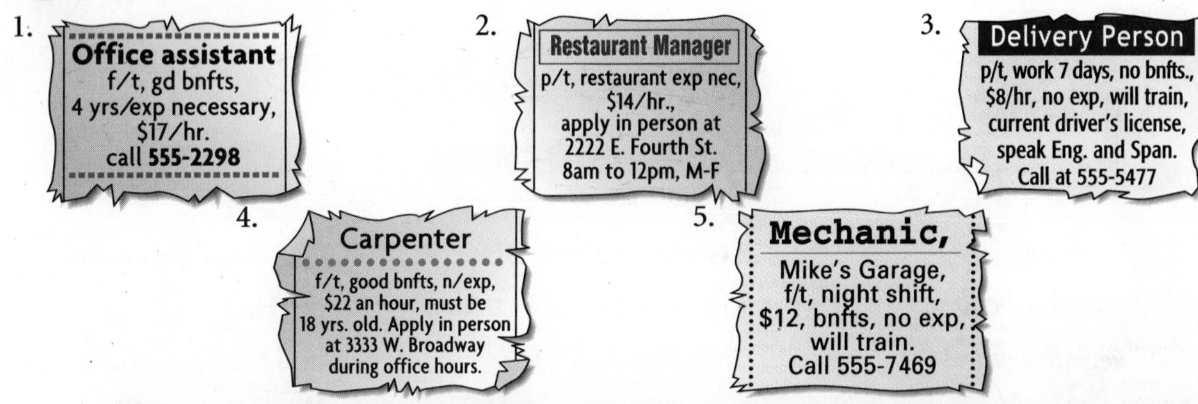
1.
Office assistant
f/t, gd bnfts,
4 yrs/exp necessary,
$17/hr.
call 555-2298
2.
Restaurant Manager
p/t, restaurant exp nec,
$14/hr.,
apply in person at
2222 E. Fourth St.
8am to 12pm, M-F
3.
Delivery Person
p/t, work 7 days, no bnfts.,
$8/hr, no exp, will train,
current driver's license,
speak Eng. and Span.
Call at 555-5477
4.
Carpenter
f/t, good bnfts, n/exp,
$22 an hour, must be
18 yrs. old. Apply in person
at 3333 W. Broadway
during office hours.
5.
Mechanic,
Mike's Garage,
f/t, night shift,
$12, bnfts, no exp,
will train.
Call 555-7469

Position	Experience?	F/T or P/T	Benefits?	Pay
1.				
2.				
3.				
4.				
5.				

C **What tools and skills do you need for these jobs?**

Job	Tools	Skill(s)
office worker		
cook		
mechanic		
student		
teacher		

D **What should you do in a job interview? What should you not do? Add sentences to this list.**

Should	Should not
You should be on time.	***You should not chew gum.***
____________________	____________________
____________________	____________________

E **Fill in the missing words with verbs from the box. Choose the present or past tense.**

be	move	have	chop	be
deliver	help	live	work	like

Francisco ____________ in Guatemala before he ____________ to California. In Guatemala, he ____________ a cook in a small fast-food restaurant. He ____________ vegetables, and ____________ in the kitchen. He ____________ fourteen hours every day and he ____________ no free time. Now he ____________ a mail carrier in California. He ____________ letters and packages. He ____________ his new job very much.

F **Underline the correct adverb or adjective for each sentence.**

1. David is a careful/carefully driver. You can feel safe in his car.
2. Anya types quick/quickly—almost 70 words per minute.
3. Eva speaks loud/loudly because she has a lot of students in her class.
4. Antonio practices English every day, and he speaks English very good/well.

G **What do these warnings mean? Write one sentence for each warning. Use *must* or *must not*.**

1. No smoking ____
2. Go slow ____
3. No parking ____
4. Head protection required ____

TEAM PROJECT

A new job

In this project you will write a pamphlet to show people how to get and keep a job.

1. Form a team with four or five students.

   In your team, you need:

Position	Job	Student Name
Student 1 Leader	See that everyone speaks English. See that everyone participates.	
Student 2 Artist	Organize the pamphlet with help from the team.	
Student 3 Writer	Write the ideas with help from the team.	
Student 4 Spokesperson	With help from the team, organize a presentation to give to the class.	

2. Write the first section of your pamphlet. What does a good employee need to do? Make a list of points, e.g., *A good employee dresses well.*
3. The next section is about looking for a job. Write an example classified ad for a position. Put it in your pamphlet.
4. Fill out an application carefully. Write an example of a job history.
5. What do you do in an interview? Write what you should and shouldn't do in an interview.
6. You should learn about the skills and equipment needed for your job. Make a list of special skills and tools needed for five different jobs.
7. Make a presentation to the class.

PRONUNCIATION

Listen to the vowel sound in these words. Underline the words with a long /e/ sound. Circle the words with a short /i/ sound. Then listen again and repeat.

speak	need	quick	teacher	build	little
listen	feel	clean	fix	fill	please

LEARNER LOG

Circle what you learned and write the page number where you learned it.

1. I can identify jobs.
   Yes Maybe No Page ______
2. I can read classified ads.
   Yes Maybe No Page ______
3. I can use the regular simple past.
   Yes Maybe No Page ______
4. I can prepare for an interview.
   Yes Maybe No Page ______
5. I can identify tools and skills at work.
   Yes Maybe No Page ______
6. I can understand warning signs at work.
   Yes Maybe No Page ______
7. I can read a work evaluation.
   Yes Maybe No Page ______
8. I can use adjectives and adverbs.
   Yes Maybe No Page ______

Did you answer *No* to any questions? Review the information with a partner.

Rank what you like to do best from 1 to 6. 1 is your favorite activity. Your teacher will help you.

- ☐ practice listening
- ☐ practice speaking
- ☐ practice reading
- ☐ practice writing
- ☐ learn new words (vocabulary)
- ☐ learn grammar

In the next unit I want to practice more

______________________________.

UNIT 8

People and Learning

GOALS

- Talk about ways to study English
- Improve your study skills
- Use *going to* for future plans
- Use *will* to talk about the future
- Make choices about your future
- Ask and answer yes/no questions
- Evaluate your study skills

LESSON 1

Learning outside the classroom

GOAL ▶ Talk about ways to study English — *Life Skill*

What is Nubar doing?
Why?

A Read about Nubar.

Nubar is an ESL student at Franklin Adult School. The school is closed for two months. Nubar wants to study. He wants to prepare for the start of the new school year. He is studying his textbook from class. He likes to review the vocabulary and the grammar.

B What are things Nubar can do to study? Make a list with a group on a separate piece of paper. Then go to other groups and add to your list.

C Read about ways to practice English.

Many people come to the United States and don't speak English. They want to learn so they can get a better job. Some students practice at work. Others practice with their families. They also keep a journal or a vocabulary notebook. Sometimes they watch TV or listen to the radio to practice listening. It's fun to find new ways of practicing English outside of class!

D Write six things you can do to practice English outside of class.

1. ______________________________
2. ______________________________
3. ______________________________
4. ______________________________
5. ______________________________
6. ______________________________

E How do you study now? Make a list and talk to a partner.

What do I do?	What does my partner do?

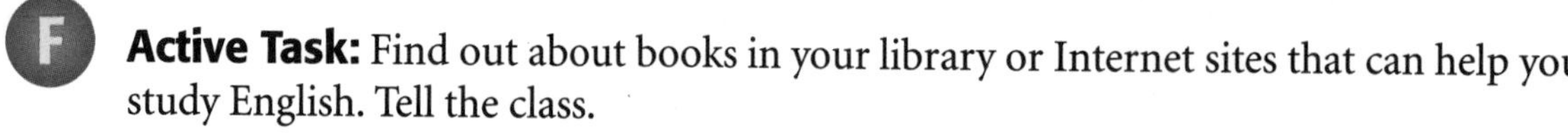

F Active Task: Find out about books in your library or Internet sites that can help you study English. Tell the class.

LESSON 2 Helping yourself learn

GOAL ▶ **Improve your study skills** — **Life Skill**

A Talk about the pictures with your teacher.

APT FOR RENT
2 bed, 1 bath apt,
818 Sundry Ave. #19.
$750, furn a/c
all utls pd 1 mth dep.
call 555-7744

be
Subject
I
Verb
am
Example sentence
I am from Mexico.

B What do you learn in English class? Write the words with the pictures.

grammar	reading	writing	life skills
speaking	vocabulary	listening	teamwork

C As a class, write other things you learn in class.

D Complete the chart.

Things I do well	Things I need help with

E **Make a notebook with sections to study at home. What are the sections in your notebook?**

vocabulary ________ ________ ________

________ ________ ________

________ ________ ________

F **Read the journal notes below.**

Date: September 5

New words: checkout, counter, cough

Skill: I practiced in the supermarket: "Where is the medicine?"

Book: I reviewed pages 10-15 in the textbook from last semester.

Listening: TV - I watched channel 20 for 10 minutes at 7 AM.

Writing: I wrote in my journal.

G **Make your own journal notes. What did you do today to practice English?**

LESSON 3 Making plans

GOAL ▶ **Use *going to* for future plans** — **Grammar**

Date: September 5

I want to make some goals. I need to prepare for school next semester. I'm going to study four pages in the textbook every weeknight for thirty minutes. I'm going to study in my kitchen at home.

A **Read Nubar's diary and answer the questions about his goals.**

1. When is Nubar going to study?

2. What is he going to study?
Four pages in the textbook.

3. Where is he going to study?

4. How long is he going to study each day?

B **What are your plans?**

1. When are you going to study?

2. What are you going to study?

3. Where are you going to study?

4. How long are you going to study each day?

Study the chart with your teacher.

going to			
Subject	***be + going to***	**Base**	**Example sentence**
I	am going to (I'm going to)	learn listen	I am going to learn English.
you, we, they	are going to (you're / we're / they're going to)	practice read speak	We are going to listen.
he, she, it	is going to (she's / he's / it's going to)	study write	She is going to write.

Look at each clock. Then listen to Nubar speak about his plans. Pretend you are Nubar. Write what you are going to do next to the clocks.

listen to the radio	read the newspaper	review my vocabulary notebook
study my textbook	write in my journal	

From to ______________________________

From to ______________________________

From to ______________________________

From to ______________________________
____

Tell a friend about Nubar's plans.

EXAMPLE: He is going to listen to the radio from 6:30 to 6:45 A.M.

F **Write sentences about Nubar's plans.**

1. *He is going to listen to the radio from 6:30 to 6:45 A.M.*
2. ______________________________
3. ______________________________
4. ______________________________

G **Write your plans.**

1. *I am going to listen to the radio from ________ to ________.*
2. ______________________________
3. ______________________________
4. ______________________________
5. ______________________________
6. ______________________________

H **Ask about the plans of four students in the class and complete the chart.**

Ask: When are you going to listen to the radio?
When are you going to practice speaking?
When are you going to read the newspaper?
When are you going to study your textbook?

Student name	Listen	Speak	Read	Study

LESSON 4 Nubar's goals

GOAL ▶ Use *will* to talk about the future — **Grammar**

What is Nubar doing?
Why is he doing it?

A Read about Nubar's goals.

Date: June 12

I have many goals for the future. Some of my goals will take a long time, but I'm going to work hard. I will study every day and get my GED. After that, I want to start college in about three years. I also want to get married and have children sometime in the future. I need a good job too, so I can help my family. I am going to be a computer technician one day.

GED = General Educational Development, the same level as a high school diploma

B Nubar wants to do many things. Write his goals in the table.

Family goals	Educational goals	Work goals
get married		

C You can use *will* to talk about future plans. Study the chart with your teacher.

will			
Subject	**Future**	**Base**	**Example sentence**
I, you, he, she, it, we, they	will	study	I will study every day.
		work	She will work hard.
		get married	They will get married.

GOAL  Use *will* to talk about the future

Grammar

D **Study these verbs and time expressions with your teacher. Make sentences about the future.**

Verbs			
to buy	to finish	to help	to move
to eat	to get	to learn	to start
to exercise	to have	to take	to study

Time expressions			
in two years	in five years	in ten years	in a few years
next week	next month	next year	sometime

E **Talk to students in the class about their future plans. Ask, *What will you do in the future?* Use the words from the chart above to write sentences about students in your class.**

Examples:
Nubar *will* start college next year.
Roberto *is going to* finish college in three years.
Gabriela *wants to* buy a house next year.

Student name	Future plan		When?
		his/her GED	
		college	
		a new job	
		a computer	
		how to use a computer	
		married	
		another city/country	

F **Write your goals and when you want to do them.**

EXAMPLES:
I am going to study next September.
I will take my GED next year.
I want to start college in three years.

____

____

____

____

G **Write a paragraph for your journal. Write about your family, educational, and work goals. Look at Nubar's journal on page 148 for some ideas.**

I have many goals for the future.

____

____

____

____

____

____

____

H **Active Task:** Start a journal. Write your goals on the first page.

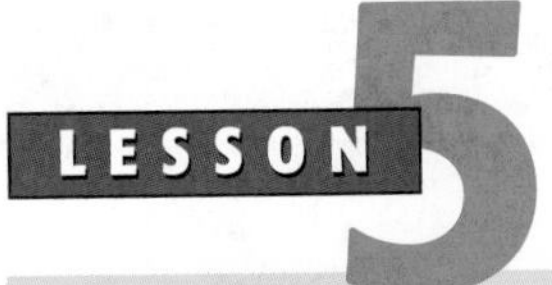

LESSON 5 Schools in the United States

GOAL ▶ **Make choices about your future** — *Life Skill*

A Read the information about these students. Listen to their conversations with a counselor. What advice does the counselor give each student? Check the choices for each student.

1. 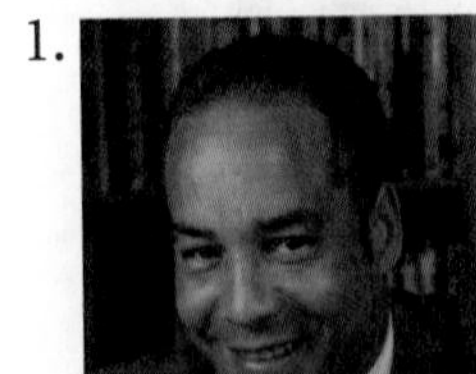

Ahmed

- ❑ high school diploma/GED
- ❑ two-year college
- ❑ university
- ❑ trade school

2. 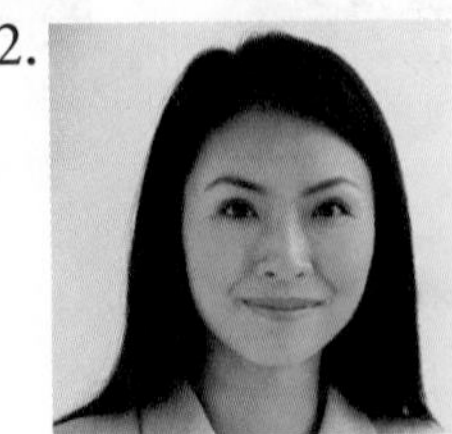

Minh

- ❑ high school diploma/GED
- ❑ two-year college
- ❑ university
- ❑ trade school

3. 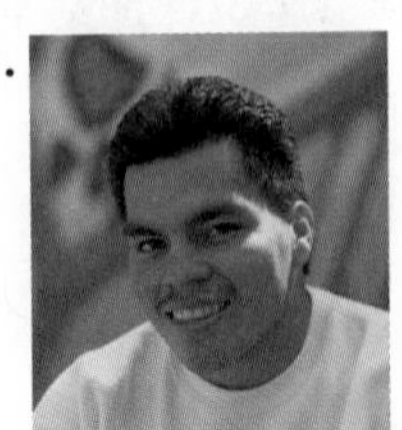

Mario

- ❑ high school diploma/GED
- ❑ two-year college
- ❑ university
- ❑ trade school

4. 

Akiko

- ❑ high school diploma/GED
- ❑ two-year college
- ❑ university
- ❑ trade school

5.

Alan

- ❑ high school diploma/GED
- ❑ two-year college
- ❑ university
- ❑ trade school

6. 

Marie

- ❑ high school diploma/GED
- ❑ two-year college
- ❑ university
- ❑ trade school

B Read about schools in the United States.

In the United States, students go to school for about twelve years and then get a high school diploma, or adults can go to an adult program to get a GED. After high school some students go to a two-year college where they prepare for a university or get an Associate's Degree. Other people go from high school to a university for four years or more. After four years, students can get a Bachelor's Degree. Some students go to trade school for one to four years after high school to learn about specific job skills.

C Talk in pairs about schools in the United States. How many years do students go to each type of school?

What are these people doing?
What advice are they getting?

D **Where can you get advice to make good choices? Talk in a group.**

For your health: ______________________________

____

For your education: ______________________________

____

For your career: ______________________________

____

E **Did you get advice from anyone this past year? Tell the group.**

I talked to ______________________________

____

____

F **Active Task:** What books or Internet sites can help you with your educational choices? Tell the class.

LESSON 6 Choosing the right job

GOAL ▶ **Ask and answer *yes/no* questions** — ***Grammar***

A counselor is going to ask you many questions to help you with your future plans. Answer the questions about yourself. Fill in the circle under *yes* or *no*.

Personal Inventory

Yes	No	
○	○	Do you have a high school diploma or GED?
○	○	Do you have good study skills?
○	○	Do you have experience?
○	○	Do you like technology (computers, machines)?
○	○	Do you like to do the same thing every day?
○	○	Do you like to handle money?
○	○	Do you like to read?
○	○	Do you like to study and to learn new things?
○	○	Do you like to listen?
○	○	Do you like to talk on the phone?
○	○	Do you like to travel?
○	○	Do you like to work with other people?
○	○	Do you like to work at night?
○	○	Do you like to work in the daytime?
○	○	Do you like to work with your hands?
○	○	Do you like your job?
○	○	Do you work now?
○	○	Do you have goals for the future?

Write sentences on a separate sheet of paper for six of your *yes* answers in exercise A.

EXAMPLE:

Yes, I do. I like technology.

C Study the charts with your teacher.

Yes/No questions			
do	**Subject**	**Base**	**Infinitive**
Do	I	like	to study?
	you	want	to travel?
	we	need	to work with your hands?
	they		to talk?
Does	he		to work alone?
	she		to handle money?
	it		to talk on the phone?
do	**Subject**	**Base**	**Noun / Adverb**
Do	I	like	technology?
	you	want	
	we	need	
	they		
Does	he	work	right now?
	she	have	a high school diploma or GED?
	it		good study skills?

D Ask a partner questions with the words below and fill in the chart.

EXAMPLE:
Student A: Do you like technology? ***Student B:*** No, I don't. / Yes, I do.

Partner's name: ______________________________

Question	Yes	No
______________________ technology?		
______________________ work alone?		
______________________ phone?		
______________________ experience?		
______________________ goals?		

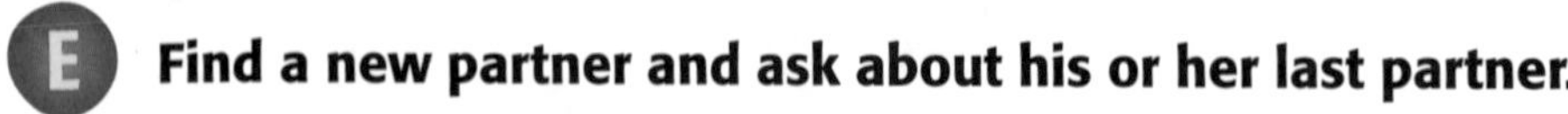

E Find a new partner and ask about his or her last partner.

EXAMPLE:
Student A: Does Cecelia like technology?
Student B: Yes, she does. / No, she doesn't.

LESSON 7 How are your study habits?

GOAL ▶ Evaluate your study skills — **Academic Skill**

A **Answer the questions about this course. Fill in the circle for each answer.**

Study Habits Questionnaire

1. How often did you come to class?
   ○ a. most of the time ○ b. more than 50% ○ c. less than 50%
2. Did you come to class on time?
   ○ a. most of the time ○ b. more than 50% ○ c. less than 50%
3. How much did you study at home each week?
   ○ a. more than 10 hours ○ b. 5-10 hours a week ○ c. less than 5 hours
4. Did you speak English in class and participate?
   ○ a. most of the time ○ b. more than 50% ○ c. less than 50%
5. Did you teach and help other students in class?
   ○ a. a lot ○ b. a little ○ c. never
6. Did you listen to the radio in English?
   ○ a. a lot ○ b. a little ○ c. never
7. Did you watch TV in English?
   ○ a. a lot ○ b. a little ○ c. never
8. Did you ask the teacher or other students questions when you didn't understand?
   ○ a. a lot ○ b. a little ○ c. never

How many *a* answers, *b* answers, and *c* answers do you have?

# of *a* answers	# of *b* answers	# of *c* answers

Do the math below.

# of *a* answers x 3 = _______
# of *b* answers x 2 = _______
# of *c* answers x 1 = _______
Total = _______

Score: 20-24 Super – You have great study habits!

Score: 16-19 Good – You have good study habits.

Score: Under 16 – You need to change your study habits!

B **Study the charts with your teacher.**

Regular verbs	
Base	**Simple past**
study	studied
participate	participated
help	helped
listen	listened
watch	watched
ask	asked

Irregular verbs	
Base	**Simple past**
come	came
see	saw
write	wrote
speak	spoke
read	read
teach	taught

C **Write sentences about what you did in this course.**

____

____

____

____

____

____

D **Review the charts about the future on pages 146 and 148 and make goals for next semester.**

EXAMPLE:
I'm going to come to school every day.

____

____

____

____

____

____

E **Active Task:** Write the goals in your journal.

Review

A **Fill in the missing words in the paragraph below.**

Degree	college	trade	diploma	twelve	four	GED

In the United States, students go to school for about ____________ years and then get a high school ____________, or adults can go to an adult program to get a ____________. After high school some students go to a two-year ____________ where they prepare for university or get an Associate's ____________. Other people go from high school to a university for ____________ years or more. Some students go to ____________ school to learn about specific job skills.

B **What are four ways to practice English outside of class?**

EXAMPLE: ***I can read the newspaper.***

1. ______________________________
2. ______________________________
3. ______________________________
4. ______________________________

C **What are three things you can do to improve your study skills?**

1. ______________________________
2. ______________________________
3. ______________________________

D **Make sentences with the words below about yourself in the future. Use *going to, want to,* or *will*.**

learn ***I'm going to learn*** ____________________

eat ***I will*** ____________________

exercise ____________________

visit ____________________

finish ____________________

get ____________________

help ____________________

find ____________________

start ____________________

study ____________________

E **What are six things you did in this course to help you study English? Use the verbs from the box.**

participate	help	speak	ask	read	listen

EXAMPLE:
I came to class every day.

1. ____________________
2. ____________________
3. ____________________
4. ____________________
5. ____________________
6. ____________________

TEAM PROJECT

My Goals

In this project you will plan your study time on a calendar. You will also write out your goals and plans in two paragraphs. You will present your calendar and your paragraphs to the class.

1. Complete a calendar for this and next month.

   Write what days and what times you are going to:

   study in the textbook
   listen to the radio
   read the newspaper
   watch TV
   practice flashcards
   write in your journal

2. Discuss your plans with your team.
3. Write a paragraph about your plans on the calendar on another piece of paper. Start your paragraph like this:

   I have many goals. I'm going to study English outside of class.

   First, . . .

4. Write another paragraph about your goals for good study habits.

   Are you going to come to school every day? Are you going to arrive on time? What else are you going to do?

5. Ask members of your team to edit your paragraphs and then rewrite them.
6. Read your paragraphs to your team.
7. As a team, design a goal chart that you can put in your home to remind you of what you want to do.
8. Present your calendar, paragraphs, and goal chart to the class.

PRONUNCIATION

Listen to the vowel sounds in these words. Circle the words that sound like *firm* and underline the words that sound like *farm*. Then listen again and repeat.

learn	start	work	park	nurse	part	heart
card	clerk	shirt	hurt	chart	journal	hurt

LEARNER LOG

Circle what you learned and write the page number where you learned it.

1. I can talk about ways to study outside of class.
   Yes Maybe No Page ______
2. I can organize a notebook and other study tools.
   Yes Maybe No Page ______
3. I can use time expressions about the future.
   Yes Maybe No Page ______
4. I can use *will* and *going to* for future plans.
   Yes Maybe No Page ______
5. I can talk about different types of schools.
   Yes Maybe No Page ______
6. I can make choices about the future.
   Yes Maybe No Page ______
7. I can ask yes/no questions.
   Yes Maybe No Page ______
8. I can evaluate my study skills.
   Yes Maybe No Page ______

Did you answer *No* to any questions? Review the information with a partner.

Rank what you like to do best from 1 to 6. 1 is your favorite activity. Your teacher will help you.

- [ ] practice listening
- [ ] practice speaking
- [ ] practice reading
- [ ] practice writing
- [ ] learn new words (vocabulary)
- [ ] learn grammar

I think I improved most in

______________________________.

Useful Words

Cardinal numbers

1	one
2	two
3	three
4	four
5	five
6	six
7	seven
8	eight
9	nine
10	ten
11	eleven
12	twelve
13	thirteen
14	fourteen
15	fifteen
16	sixteen
17	seventeen
18	eighteen
19	nineteen
20	twenty
21	twenty-one
30	thirty
40	forty
50	fifty
60	sixty
70	seventy
80	eighty
90	ninety
100	one hundred
1000	one thousand
10,000	ten thousand
100,000	one hundred thousand
1,000,000	one million

Ordinal numbers

first	1st
second	2nd
third	3rd
fourth	4th
fifth	5th
sixth	6th
seventh	7th
eighth	8th
ninth	9th
tenth	10th
eleventh	11th
twelfth	12th
thirteenth	13th
fourteenth	14th
fifteenth	15th
sixteenth	16th
seventeenth	17th
eighteenth	18th
nineteenth	19th
twentieth	20th
twenty-first	21st

Days of the week

Sunday
Monday
Tuesday
Wednesday
Thursday
Friday
Saturday

Seasons

winter
spring
summer
fall

Months of the year

January
February
March
April
May
June
July
August
September
October
November
December

Write the date

April 5, 2004 = 4/ 5/ 04

Temperature chart

Degrees Celsius (°C) and
Degrees Fahrenheit (°F)

°C	°F
100°C	212°F
30°C	86°F
25°C	77°F
20°C	68°F
15°C	59°F
10°C	50°F
5°C	41°F
0°C	32°F
−5°C	23°F

Weights and measures

Weight:
1 pound (lb.) = 453.6 grams (g)
16 ounces (oz.) = 1 pound (lb.)
1 pound (lb.) = .45 kilogram (kg)

Liquid or Volume:
1 cup (c.) = .24 liter (l)
2 cups (c.) = 1 pint (pt.)
2 pints = 1 quart (qt.)
4 quarts = 1 gallon (gal.)
1 gallon (gal.) = 3.78 liters (l)

Length:
1 inch (in. or ″) = 2.54 centimeters (cm)
1 foot (ft. or ′) = .3048 meters (m)
12 inches (12″) = 1 foot (1′)
1 yard (yd.) = 3 feet (3′) or 0.9144 meters (m)
1 mile (mi.) = 1609.34 meters (m) or 1.609 kilometers (km)

Time:
60 seconds = 1 minute
60 minutes = 1 hour
24 hours = 1 day
28–31 days = 1 month
12 months = 1 year

Grammar Reference

The Simple Present – *be*		
Subject	**Verb**	**Example sentence**
I	am ('m)	I am (I'm) Roberto.
you, we, they he, she, it	are ('re) is ('s)	You are (You're) a student. We are (We're) happy.
		She is (She's) from Mexico.

The Simple Present – *be* (negative)		
Subject	**Verb**	**Example sentence**
I	am ('m) not	I am not (I'm not) hungry.
you, we, they	are ('re) not	You are not (aren't) from Mexico.
he, she, it	is ('s) not	She is not (isn't) a student.

The Simple Present – *have*		
Subject	**Verb**	**Example sentence**
I, you, we, they	have	I have three brothers. We have a cat.
he, she, it	has	He has free time. She has black hair.

The Simple Present – *have* (negative)			
Subject	***do* + *not***	**Verb**	**Example sentence**
I, you, we, they	do not (don't)	have	I do not (don't) have children. We do not (don't) have a dog.
he , she, it	does not (doesn't)		He does not (doesn't) have blond hair.

The Simple Present – *Regular verbs*		
Subject	**Verb**	**Object**
I, you, we, they	bring eat like	sandwiches lunch green salad
he, she, it	brings eats likes	

The Simple Present – *Regular verbs* (negative)			
Subject	***do* + *not***	**Verb**	**Object**
I, you, we, they	do not (don't)	bring eat like	sandwiches lunch green salad
he, she, it	does not (doesn't)		

The Simple Present (yes/no question forms with *do*)				
do	**Subject**	**Base**	**Object**	**Example question**
do	I, you, we, they	like	technology	Do you like technology?
does	he, she, it	have	a diploma	Does he have a diploma?

The Simple Past – *be*		
Subject	**Past**	**Example sentence**
I, he, she, it	was	He was a mail carrier.
you, we, they	were	They were in the office.

The Simple Past – *Regular verbs*			
Subject	**Base**	**Base + *ed***	**Example sentence**
I, you, he, she, it, we, they	clean	cleaned	I cleaned tables.
	cook	cooked	You cooked hamburgers.
	prepare	prepared	He prepared breakfast.

The Present Continuous			
Subject	**be**	**Base + *ing***	**Example sentence**
I	am	calling	I am calling about the apartment.
you, we, they	are	working	They are looking for a house.
he, she , it	is	looking	She is working right now.

Imperative form		
(You)	**Base**	**Example sentence**
	chop	Chop the potatoes.

Imperative form (negative)			
(You)	***do + not (don't)***	**Base**	**Example sentence**
	do not (don't)	boil	Do not (don't) boil the water.

Modal Verbs (affirmative and negative forms)			
Subject	**Modal**	**Base**	**Example sentence**
I, you, he, she, it, we, they	should should not (shouldn't)	rest go out	He should rest. You should not (shouldn't) go out.
I, you, he, she, it, we, they	can cannot (can't)	drive type	I can drive. She cannot (can't) type.
I, you, he, she, it, we, they	must must not	wear enter	You must wear eye protection. We must not enter this area.
I, you, he, she, it, we, they	will will not (won't)	study move	They will study English next year. He will not (won't) move to Florida.

The Modal Verb – should (*Wh-* question form)				
Question word	**Modal**	**Subject**	**Base**	**Example question**
What	should	I, you, he, she, it, we, they	do?	What should I do?

Verb + infinitive				
Subject	**Verb**	**Infinitive (*to* + base)**		**Example sentence**
I, you, we, they	want	to	exercise	I want to exercise.
he, she, it	wants		walk	She wants to walk.

Future–*going to*			
Subject	***be + going to***	**Base**	**Example sentence**
I	am going to	be	I am going to be a mechanic.
you, we, they	are going to	work	You are going to work hard.
he, she, it	is going to	save	She is going to save money.

Possessive adjectives		
Subject pronoun	**Possessive adjective**	**Example sentence**
I	my	*My* shirt is blue. *My* shoes are black.
you	your	*Your* baseball cap is blue. *Your* shorts are brown.
he	his	*His* belt is black. *His* sandals are brown.
she	her	*Her* blouse is pink. *Her* shoes are white.
it	its	*Its* label is red. *Its* doors are green.
we	our	*Our* house is white. *Our* books are blue.
they	their	*Their* school is in Center City. *Their* children are happy.

Demonstrative adjectives			
	Near the speaker	**Away from the speaker**	**Example sentence**
Singular	this	that	I want *this* umbrella and *that* cap.
Plural	these	those	I want *these* jeans and *those* socks.

Stand Out 1 Vocabulary List

eyes 101
foot (feet) 101
hand 101
head 101
leg 101
mouth 101
nose 101
stomach 101
throat 101
tooth (teeth) 101

Unit 6
Health
ambulance 111
aspirin 105
cold 103
cough 103
emergency 111
fever 103
flu 103
headache 103
lozenges 105
muscle ache 103
runny nose 103
sore throat 103
syrup 105
temperature 104

Unit 7
Jobs
artist 122
busboy 125
cook 125
homemaker 122
mail carrier 125
mechanic 121
nurse 121
office worker 121
server 121
Employment
application 123
benefits 123
experience 123
full-time 123
insurance 123
interview 128
part-time 123
sick leave 123
vacation 123
Work tools
broom 130
computer 130
copier 130
hammer 130
mop 130
phone 130
saw 130
wrench 130
Work verbs
build 131
deliver 131
drive 131
fix 131
manage 131
sweep 131
type 131

Unit 8
Education
adult program 151
Associate's Degree 151
Bachelor's Degree 151
college 151
counselor 151
degree 157
diploma 148
GED (General Educational Development) 148
goal 148
trade school 151
university 151

Stand Out 1 Irregular Verb List

The verbs below are used in *Stand Out 1* and have irregular past tense forms.

Base verb	Simple past	Base verb	Simple past
be	was, were	give	gave
bring	brought	go	went
build	built	have	had
buy	bought	make	made
choose	chose	meet	met
come	came	put	put
do	did	read	read
drive	drove	see	saw
drink	drank	send	sent
draw	drew	sleep	slept
eat	ate	speak	spoke
feel	felt	teach	taught
find	found	write	wrote

Stand Out 1 Listening Scripts

Pre-Unit

p. P3, Lesson 2, exercise C
1. Hi! I'm Susan. S-U-S-A-N
2. Hello! My name's Bill. B-I-L-L
3. How are you? I'm Annette. A-N-N-E-T-T-E
4. Hi! My name's Tony. T-O-N-Y

p. P4, Lesson 3, exercise C
a. five b. eight c. nine d. three e. zero f. ten

p. P4, Lesson 3, exercise E
My name is Gabriela. My address is 14 Main Street. The zip code is 06119. The phone number is 401-555-7248. There are sixteen students in my class.

p. P5, Lesson 5, exercise C
1. Please stand up.
2. Please sit down.
3. Please read page one in your book.
4. Please take out a piece of paper.
5. Please listen carefully.
6. Please write your name on the paper.

Unit 1

p. 2, Lesson 1, exercise C

A. Roberto is a new student in Beginning English at President Adult School. Roberto and his family are from Mexico City, Mexico.

B. Eva Malinska is happy to be in the United States. She wants to learn English. In Warsaw, Poland, she learned a bit of English. She wants to help other people in her family learn the language.

C. Gabriela Ramirez is 26. She listens to the radio and reads the newspaper every day in English. She wants to learn quickly. She's from Buenos Aires, Argentina.

D. Duong is a new student. He speaks Vietnamese. Now Duong goes to school to learn English. Duong wants to go to college.

p. 4, Lesson 2, exercise A
Tatsuya: Excuse me. Is it OK to interview you?
Felipe: Sounds good. Go ahead.
Tatsuya: What's your first name?
Felipe: My first name is Felipe. F-E-L-I-P-E
Tatsuya: Where are you from?
Felipe: I'm from Cuba.
Tatsuya: Are you married or single?
Felipe: I'm single.
Tatsuya: How old are you?
Felipe: Twenty-three years old.
Tatsuya: Thanks, Felipe.
Felipe: No problem.

p. 4, Lesson 2, exercise C
My name is Tatsuya. This is my new friend, Felipe. Felipe is from Cuba. He is 23 years old. He is single. We are students in this class.

p. 11, Lesson 5, exercise C
My name is Roberto Garcia. I am very happily married. My wife's name is Silvia. This is a picture of my family. The older man and woman in the picture are my parents. My mother's name is Rebecca and my father's name is Antonio. I have one sister, Lidia, and one brother, Julio. The girl and boy are my children, Juan and Carla.

p. 13, Lesson 6, exercise A
Roberto and Silvia are happily married. Roberto likes movies, games, and books. Silvia likes parks, restaurants, and music. They both like sports, computers, and TV.

Unit 2

p. 22, Lesson 1, exercise D
Van: I need some things for school. Do you want to shop with me?
Nam: No, not today. I have things to do here at home.
Van: OK. Where can I go for all these things?
Nam: What do you need?
Van: I need sneakers, shirts, fruit, bread and cheese for lunches, a CD player, and a bilingual dictionary.
Nam: Wow, it sounds like a lot.
Van: I know.
Nam: The best place for shoes is Martin's Department Store. You can buy shirts at Martin's also. You can probably also buy a good CD player at Martin's.
Van: All at Martin's?
Nam: Yes, it's a good place for many things, but I think you need to go to Hero's Bookstore for the dictionary. You know Sam's Food Mart around the corner has all you need for your lunches.

p. 23, Lesson 2, exercise C
Ex. How much is it? It's $22.50.
1. That's $34.15, please.
2. Here's $33.
3. That comes to $15.70.
4. The total cost is $77.95.

p. 23, Lesson 2, exercise D

1. Customer: Excuse me. How much is this vacuum?
   Salesperson: It's $98.99 on sale.
   Customer: Thanks, I'll take it.

2. Customer: Excuse me. Can you help me? I'm looking for a washing machine.
   Salesperson: This is a good brand.
   Customer: Is that right? OK, how much is it?
   Salesperson: It's 450 dollars.
   Customer: Four hundred and fifty dollars? That much?
   Salesperson: I'm afraid so.

3. Customer: I want to buy a ream of white paper.
   Salesperson: The paper is over there. It's $6.50.
   Customer: Thank you.

4. Customer: I just want this candy bar.
   Salesperson: That will be $1.25 please.
   Customer: Here you go. One dollar and twenty-five cents.

5. Customer: Every time I buy a phone, I get a bad one. Maybe I should buy an expensive one.
   Salesperson: How about this one for $80?

p. 34, Lesson 7, exercise A
Part one
Roberto: Excuse me, I need a cap and an umbrella.
Salesperson: Yes, sir. How about that yellow cap over there?
Roberto: No, I prefer this orange cap.
Salesperson: OK, and how about this umbrella?
Roberto: No, it's too dark. I like that red umbrella.

Part two
Roberto: I really need some jeans and some socks, too.
Salesperson: We have blue jeans and black jeans. How about those blue jeans?
Roberto: Yes, they look good. And a pair of these socks, please.
Salesperson: Great. I'll ring it all up.
Roberto: Thank you.

p. 37, Review, exercise A
The tape player is $98.45 with tax; The shirt is $24.50; The TV is 456.78; The vacuum is $168.00; The shoes are $28.98; The dictionary is $18.95; The sweater is $33.99; The shorts are $17.00.

Unit 3

p. 43, Lesson 2, exercise A
Alex: Can I buy you lunch Natasha?
Natasha: No, but you can help me. How do you work this thing anyway?
Alex: First you decide what you want. Next, put your money here.
Natasha: I only have two dollars.
Alex: That's OK, the sandwiches are $1.75.
Natasha: OK, I want the tuna sandwich.
Alex: Put your dollar bills in this slot face up so the president is looking away from you.
Natasha: What is face up?
Alex: So the president is looking up.
Natasha: I see.
Alex: Choose the number and take your change.
Natasha: Thank you, Alex. Maybe next time you can buy me lunch.
Alex: I'd love to.

p. 45, Lesson 3, exercise B
1. Sebastien: I want a cheeseburger and an orange juice, please.
   Server: No orange juice today. Milk? Cola?
   Sebastien: A cola, please.
   Server: OK, two minutes. Next.

2. Tran: What sandwiches do you have?
   Server: Ham or cheese.
   Tran: I'll have a ham sandwich.
   Server: OK.
   Tran: And a green salad, too.
   Server: Of course. What about a drink?
   Tran: No, thanks.
   Server: OK, that's a ham sandwich and a green salad, right?
   Tran: That's right, thanks.

3. Miyuki: I want some milk, please, and a hot dog.
   Server: Do you want mustard?
   Miyuki: No, thanks. Just French fries.
   Server: That's fine. Hot dog, no mustard, French fries, and milk coming up.

p. 51, Lesson 5, exercise F
Duong: We need to go shopping. We are out of everything.
Minh: You're right. Let's make a shopping list.
Duong: Well, I know we need ground beef.
Minh: That's not all. We really need carrots and tomatoes, too.
Duong: OK, I'll write that down, carrots and tomatoes.
Minh: I never buy any spaghetti or milk because you don't like them, but let's buy some cola. OK?
Duong: OK. I'll add it to the list.
Minh: We don't need peanut butter . . .
Duong: Avocados are expensive but let's buy two?
Minh: That's fine.
Duong: That should be the whole list. I have ground beef, carrots, tomatoes, cola, and avocados on the list.

Unit 4

p. 63, Lesson 2, exercise A
1. Saud: I'm looking for a house to rent for my family.
   Agent: Would you please sit down?
   Saud: Thank you.
   Agent: How many bedrooms do you need?
   Saud: I need three bedrooms and one bathroom.
   Agent: I think we can help you.

2. Silvia: We're interested in a nice apartment in the city.
   Agent: I'm sure we can help you. This one has two bathrooms and two bedrooms. Is that OK?
   Silvia: Maybe. What's the rent?
   Agent: It's only $850 a month.
   Silvia: $850 a month? This is going to be more difficult than I thought.

3. Tien: Do you have any properties for a big family?
   Agent: Well, let's see.
   Tien: I think I need a house with four bedrooms.
   Agent: To rent or buy?
   Tien: To rent, I think. How much are the rentals here?
   Agent: We have one here with two bathrooms for $1300 a month.
   Tien: Can we go out and look at it?
   Agent: Yes, of course.

4. Felipe: What do you have in a one-bedroom?
   Agent: We have this one-bedroom on Sycamore Street.
   Felipe: That looks great. How much is the rent?
   Agent: It's $750 a month, plus utilities.
   Felipe: Is it one bathroom too?
   Agent: That's right, one bathroom and one bedroom.

p. 66, Lesson 3, exercise D
1. This apartment is a large three-bedroom with lots of good features. There is also a pool. All the utilities are paid and it's near a school. Come and visit. You won't be sorry.
2. Apartments come and go, but this is the best. It has three bedrooms and it's only $800 a month. It's on the second floor so you can enjoy a beautiful balcony.
3. This great home is far from the city traffic. Hot summers are no problem. We have air conditioning and we pay the electricity. Call Margaret at 555-5678.
4. This is a bargain! $700 a month on a lease for this one-bedroom one-bath small apartment. No pets please! Call our manager Fred. He will get you in today! 555-7164.

Unit 5

p. 85, Lesson 3, exercise B
Ex. A: Excuse me. I'm looking for the mall. Do you know if it's close by?
    B: Yes it is. Turn around and then turn right on Broadway. You can't miss it. There are signs all over.
    A: OK, turn around and then turn right on Broadway.
    B: That's right. It's only a mile away.

1. A: I'm new here and need to find the post office to mail a package. Can you give me directions?
   B: Yes, that's easy. Go straight about a block. It's only a half mile away on this street.
   A: That's great, thank you.

2. A: Let's go to the movies.
   B: I can't go right now. I'm waiting for a friend to come over.
   A: Why don't you and your friend meet us there?
   B: OK, how do you get there?
   A: From here you need to turn around and go to Nutwood. Turn right on Fairview. The Movieplex Theaters are on Fairview, not too far down.
   B: Great. We'll see you there. What time?
   A: I think the movie starts at eight.

3. A: I'm looking for the Museum of Aviation. Do you know where it is?
   B: Yes. It's a little far. It's down on Main, downtown.
   A: Downtown?
   B: Yes, turn right on Center Street, then left on Main. Go about five miles on Main. You'll see it close to the police station.

4. A: Excuse me. Where is Monterey Park? Do you know?
   B: I think so. It's not a very big park. I think it's in the residential area on Boulder Lane.
   A: Oh, now I understand. I was looking on main streets.
   B: Turn left at the next street. Then turn right. Go straight ahead for two blocks and you will see it by a school.
   A: Thanks. I hope I find it this time.
   B: Good luck.

p. 90, Lesson 5, exercise B
A. This is a place where people mail letters and packages and buy stamps. It is a government agency.

B. This is a place with trained workers who help the community when there is an emergency like a fire.

C. This is a place where very sick people go for surgery and other problems. Sometimes people go here in an emergency. They sometimes come by ambulance.

D. This is where people go to get a driver's license and identification.

E. This is a place where people put their money. Sometimes they get a checking account and sometimes they get credit cards and loans.

F. This is a place where police officers work. It is the police officers' office.

p. 92, Lesson 6, exercise C
Machine: Hello, this is David. I can't come to the phone right now, but your call is very important. Please leave a message after the tone and I will get back to you right away. Beeep.
Gabriela: This is Gabriela. I want to go to the post office tomorrow. Can you go with me? I hope so. I need some help from a friend.

p. 98, Review, exercise C
Ex. Machine: This is Herman. I can't come to the phone right now. Please, leave a message. Beeeep.
Nadia: This is Nadia. I have a question. My number is 555–2344.

1. Machine: This is Herman. I can't come to the phone right now. Please, leave a message. Beeeep.
Vien: This is Vien. I want to talk. Can you call me? My number is 555–7798.

2. Machine: This is Herman. I can't come to the phone right now. Please, leave a message. Beeeep.
David: David here. I need information. Please call 555–1069.

3. Machine: This is Herman. I can't come to the phone right now. Please, leave a message. Beeeep.
Ricardo: My name is Ricardo. I need a phone number. My number is 555–7343.

Unit 6

p. 102, Lesson 1, exercise C
1. Karen: Doctor, thank you for seeing me on such short notice.
Doctor: What seems to be the trouble?
Karen: Well I'm having trouble with my hand.
Doctor: What do you mean, trouble?
Karen: My hand is very stiff in the morning. I work at a computer and it is getting very difficult to do my work.

2. Doctor: How are you today, Roberto?
Roberto: I'm fine, except my leg hurts all the time.
Doctor: I see. Let's check it out. Where does it hurt?
Roberto: My leg hurts right here near the knee.
Doctor: We probably should take some X-rays.

3. Vien: Doctor, I have a terrible earache.
Doctor: Does it hurt all the time?
Vien: Yes, but especially when I am outside.
Doctor: Hmm. You may have some kind of infection.

4. Doctor: Well, Tino, it seems like you are here every week these days.
Tino: I guess so, doctor. My feet are killing me!
Doctor: I know that you were here last week because of your elbow. Didn't the prescription help?
Tino: Not at all. It seems to be getting worse.

5. Eric: Doctor, I really need your help.
Doctor: What can I do for you?
Eric: My stomach starts to hurt after I eat anything.
Doctor: Well, let's see if we can find something to help you with that.

p. 108, Lesson 4, exercise B
A. Doctor: Now Karen, I know you are in pain. You will need some medicine to help you. I'm writing a prescription for a pain reliever. Please be careful and keep it away from your children.
Karen: OK, doctor, I will keep it out of my children's reach.

B. Doctor: You should take two tablets every four hours during the day.
Karen: Yes, OK.
Doctor: It is very important that you don't take too much. Follow the directions carefully and don't take more than two tablets every four hours. OK?
Karen: Yes, doctor, I understand.

C. Doctor: It's not good to take this medication if you are expecting a baby.
Karen: It's OK, I'm not pregnant.

D. Doctor: This medicine will make you a little tired. Be careful when driving.
Karen: OK, maybe I shouldn't drive at all, to be safe.

p. 110, Lesson 5, exercise C
Ex. Operator: 911. What is your emergency?
Rodrigo: There is a fire at 9235 W. Brookfield and I think someone is inside.
Operator: What's your name?
Rodrigo: Rodrigo Sandoval. Please hurry.
Operator: We will send the fire department and the paramedics out immediately.

1. Operator: 911. What is your emergency?
Anya: We have a medical emergency here.
Operator: What's happened?
Anya: A woman here at work is having a heart attack.
Operator: Is she conscious?
Anya: Yes, but she is holding her chest in pain.
Operator: What is the address?
Anya: 45 Center Street.
Operator: The ambulance will be there very soon.

2. Operator: 911. What is your emergency?
Felipe: There's a car accident on Murphy and Garden Ave.
Operator: Are there injuries?
Felipe: Maybe.
Operator: What's your name?
Felipe: Felipe Perez.
Operator: Felipe, the police and the paramedics are coming.

3. Operator: 911. What is your emergency?
Brian: My name is Brian Jenkins and there is a man in the house next door.
Operator: You mean there is a robbery?
Brian: Yes, I think so. It's at 2546 Maple Way.
Operator: Thank you, sir. The police will be there right away.

Unit 7

p. 123, Lesson 2, exercise B
1. Manager: Roberto, you need to take your vacation right away.
Roberto: Well, I'm not sure that I have time.
Manager: If you don't take vacation now, then you will lose it. You have five days.
Roberto: OK, I'll talk to my wife and see what she says.

2. Anya: I have a problem.
Supervisor: What can I do for you?
Anya: My husband had an accident.
Supervisor: An accident? What happened?
Anya: He had a small car accident and he broke his leg.

Supervisor: What can I do?
Anya: Is he covered by my insurance?
Supervisor: Of course. Your family is all covered by your insurance.

3. Steve: I'm sorry, I have to call in sick.
Manager: I'm sorry to hear that.
Steve: Yes, I have a fever. Maybe I have the flu.
Manager: How long will you be out?
Steve: Do you know how much sick leave I have left?
Manager: I'll check on it for you.

p. 129, Lesson 4, exercise C

1. Miyuki: Excuse me. I'm interested in a job. Do you have any openings?
Manager: Not right now, but we can keep your name on file.
Miyuki: OK, can I have an application, please?

2. Miyuki: Here is my application. Can I see the manager?
Worker: Not just now, she is busy.
Miyuki: Can I make an appointment please?

3. Manager: Are you interested in a job as a clerk?
Miyuki: Yes, that's right.
Manager: Do you have any experience?
Miyuki: No, but I'm good at math and I learn quickly.

4. Miyuki: I want to make an appointment to see the manager.
Worker: Just a moment, I'll see if she's free.
Miyuki: Thanks, I'll wait here.

p. 132, Lesson 6, exercise B

1. This is our manufacturing area. Be sure to always wear a hard hat here because sometimes metal falls from above.
2. Never enter here. This room is for photography development and you could ruin a day's work if you come in at the wrong time.
3. Our factory does not permit smoking anywhere except outside. There are many hazardous chemicals.
4. These machines could hurt your hands, so keep your hands far away from danger.
5. Keep this area clear. We need plenty of room here for cars to pass.
6. Always put this sign up after the restrooms are cleaned because it does get very slippery when wet. We don't want accidents.

Unit 8

p. 146, Lesson 3, exercise D

I want to learn English when there is no school, so I'm going to study a lot. I'm making goals so I can remember my plans. I'm going to study every weekday. When I wake up in the morning, I'm going to listen to the radio in English from 6:30 to 6:45. I'm going to listen to the news. Maybe I won't understand, but I can listen and try. From 7:00 A.M. to 7:30 A.M., I'm going to read the newspaper. I'm going to look for words that I understand. After work at night, I'm going to study four pages in the textbook from 8:00 to 8:45. From 9:00 P.M. to 9:15 P.M. I'm going to review my vocabulary notebook and then write in my journal.

p. 151, Lesson 5, exercise A

1. Ahmed: I want to be a computer technician, but first I need to learn more English.
Counselor: That's very important. Do you have a high school diploma?
Ahmed: No, I don't.
Counselor: Well, that is always a good place to start. Maybe you can get work without it, but it is very important.
Ahmed: Yes, I know. That's one of my plans.
Counselor: You can learn to be a computer technician in a trade school, or you can go to a two-year college.
Ahmed: Which one is better?
Counselor: They are both good, but a trade school will help you find a job when you finish.

2. Counselor: That's great that you want to be a teacher.
Minh: Yes, but I do need to learn English.
Counselor: That's right. You have your high school diploma, so you can start at a two-year college or go right to the university.
Minh: Which is better for me?
Counselor: They are both good. The college is cheaper and you can take English classes while you take other classes.

3. Mario: I just need a little English and I can go to work. I'm already a good mechanic.
Counselor: Do you have a GED or high school diploma?
Mario: No, do I really need one?
Counselor: A GED can really help. A good mechanic has to read instructions and manuals.
Mario: Thanks, I'm going to think about it.

4. Akiko: I want to understand computers in the United States so I can get a good job in web design.
Counselor: First, you have to speak English very well.
Akiko: If I study at home and come to this adult school, I think that will be enough.
Counselor: You should plan to go to college and take technology courses too. It's hard, but you need the experience.

5. Counselor: Alan, you want to be a cook, right?
Alan: That's right.
Counselor: Do you want to be a chef in an expensive restaurant where you can make special food?
Alan: I don't know. I like to cook. Is it hard to be a chef?
Counselor: You need to go to school – maybe a trade school.
Alan: That sounds like a lot of work, but I'll think about it.

6. Counselor: Nursing is a good job. You can take special courses at the state college.
Marie: I already have plans to go to the college here in town. Do I need to be a citizen?
Counselor: No, but you do need to be a state resident or it will cost you a lot of money.
Marie: Good, I am a state resident.

Stand Out 1 Skills Index

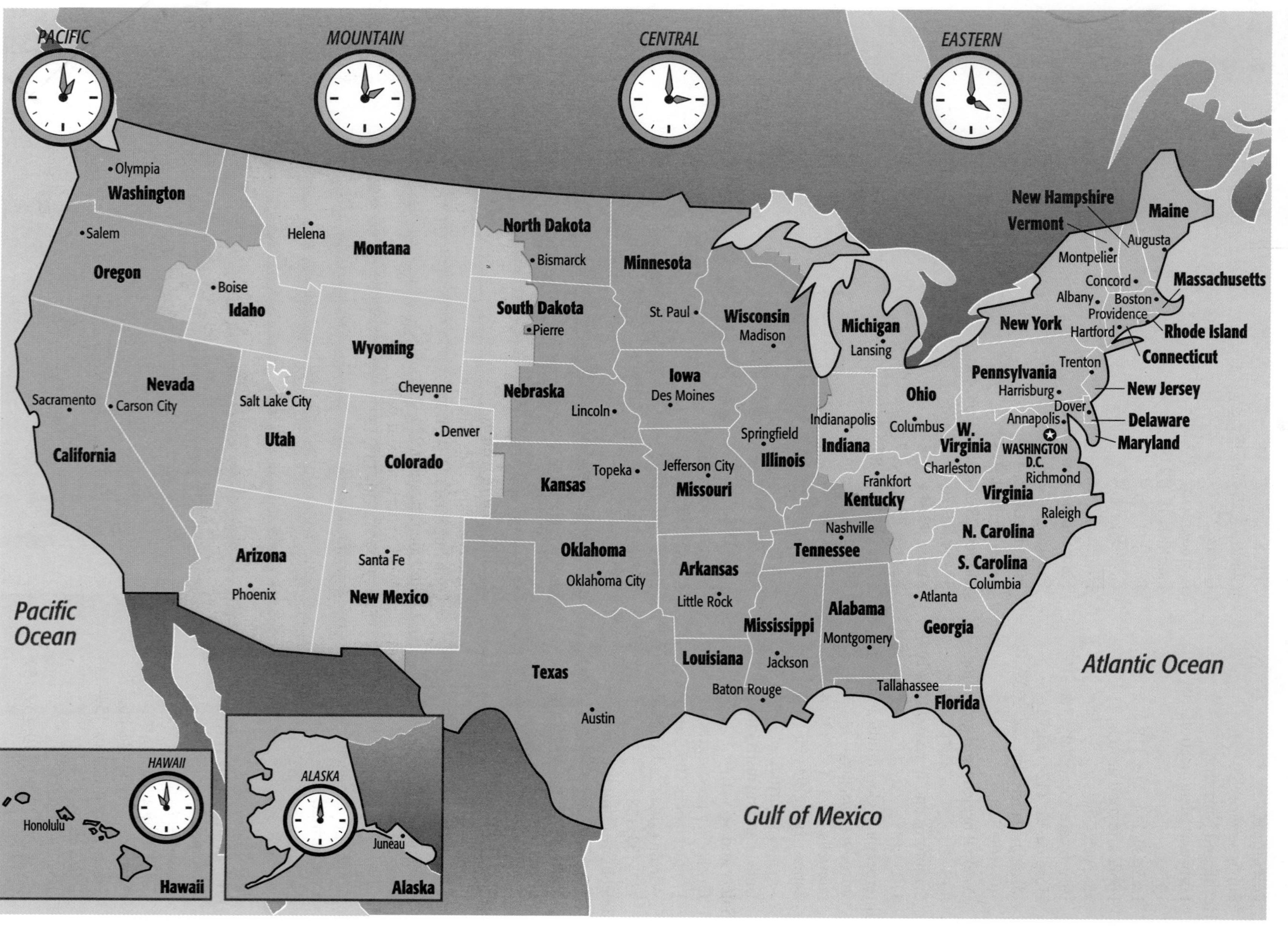
PACIFIC
MOUNTAIN
CENTRAL
EASTERN
Washington
Olympia
Oregon
Salem
California
Sacramento
Nevada
Carson City
Idaho
Boise
Montana
Helena
Wyoming
Cheyenne
Utah
Salt Lake City
Colorado
Denver
Arizona
Phoenix
New Mexico
Santa Fe
North Dakota
Bismarck
South Dakota
Pierre
Nebraska
Lincoln
Kansas
Topeka
Oklahoma
Oklahoma City
Texas
Austin
Minnesota
St. Paul
Iowa
Des Moines
Missouri
Jefferson City
Arkansas
Little Rock
Louisiana
Baton Rouge
Wisconsin
Madison
Illinois
Springfield
Michigan
Lansing
Indiana
Indianapolis
Kentucky
Frankfort
Tennessee
Nashville
Mississippi
Jackson
Alabama
Montgomery
Ohio
Columbus
W. Virginia
Charleston
Virginia
Richmond
N. Carolina
Raleigh
S. Carolina
Columbia
Georgia
Atlanta
Florida
Tallahassee
Pennsylvania
Harrisburg
New York
Albany
New Jersey
Trenton
Delaware
Dover
Maryland
Annapolis
WASHINGTON D.C.
Connecticut
Hartford
Rhode Island
Providence
Massachusetts
Boston
Vermont
Montpelier
New Hampshire
Concord
Maine
Augusta
Pacific Ocean
Atlantic Ocean
Gulf of Mexico
HAWAII
Honolulu
Hawaii
ALASKA
Juneau
Alaska